"If you want more freedom and fun, purpo[se]
Christian life, read this book!"

Comeback: An ...

"Anyone can lead someone to Christ after reading *The Insider*. It empowers and enables you with a foundation and framework to share the gospel."

—RANDY FRAZEE, pastor of Pantego Bible Church,
Fort Worth, Texas; author,
The Connecting Church: Beyond Small Groups to Authentic Community

The INSIDER

BRINGING THE KINGDOM *of* GOD
INTO YOUR EVERYDAY WORLD

*

JIM PETERSEN &
MIKE SHAMY

NAVPRESS
Discipleship Inside Out™

Discipleship Inside Out™

NavPress is the publishing ministry of The Navigators, an international Christian organization and leader in personal spiritual development. NavPress is committed to helping people grow spiritually and enjoy lives of meaning and hope through personal and group resources that are biblically rooted, culturally relevant, and highly practical.

For a free catalog go to www.NavPress.com
or call 1.800.366.7788 in the United States or 1.800.839.4769 in Canada.

Cover Design: David Carlson
Cover Image: Getty Images / Patrick Molnar
Creative Team: Don Simpson, Nat Akin, Darla Hightower, Pat Reinheimer

Some of the anecdotal illustrations in this book are true to life and are included with the permission of the persons involved. All other illustrations are composites of real situations, and any resemblance to people living or dead is coincidental.

Unless otherwise identified, all Scripture quotations in this publication are taken from the HOLY BIBLE: NEW INTERNATIONAL VERSION® (NIV®). Copyright © 1973, 1978, 1984 by International Bible Society. Used by permission of Zondervan Publishing House. All rights reserved. Other versions used include: the *New American Standard Bible* (NASB), © The Lockman Foundation 1960, 1962, 1963, 1968, 1971, 1972, 1973, 1975, 1977; *The Message: New Testament with Psalms and Proverbs* by Eugene H. Peterson, copyright © 1993, 1994, 1995, used by permission of NavPress Publishing Group; and the *Amplified New Testament* (AMP), © The Lockman Foundation 1954, 1958.

Petersen, Jim.
  The insider : bringing the Kingdom of God into your everyday world /
Jim Petersen and Mike Shamy.
    p. cm.
Includes bibliographical references.
  ISBN 1-57683-338-0
  1. Christian life. I. Shamy, Mike, 1951- II. Title.
  BV4501.3 .P47 2003
  248'.5--dc21
                                        2003014554

Printed in the United States of America

7 8 9 10 11 12 13 14 / 15 14 13 12 11

*To Lorne Sanny — who provoked our search to grasp the concept of
"the priesthood of every believer" through his persistent teaching
on the need for laborers for the harvest.*

TABLE OF CONTENTS

PREFACE

* * *

Over the past thirty to forty years, both of us, Mike and Jim, have worked alongside men and women of many cultures. Many of them share the common desire to see the "good news of the kingdom of God" advance among their families, friends, coworkers, fellow students—in short, among the people closest to them. They long for this, but they don't know how to proceed.

These are ordinary people with an extraordinary desire. They are strategically positioned as insiders—all over the world—each within a unique network of relationships, each with a key part to play in God's purposes. But what they have been taught about sharing their faith usually doesn't fit life as it really is. They often feel frustrated.

This book is an effort to serve these people. They need and deserve help in turning their vision into reality. Because both of us have enjoyed the privilege of giving our undivided attention to the growth of the gospel for many years, we have a sense of debt to these men and women. You may be one of them. If so, we feel we owe it to you to share the things we are learning along the way. What you will see on these pages is an attempt to communicate, in practical form, some of the lessons we have learned from the Scriptures and our experience. We will consider this effort a success if, when you put the book down, you think to yourself, "Is that all there is to it? I can do that!" We will consider our efforts *wildly* successful when you then act upon what you've read!

A word about the way we have written this book. Although we have both contributed to the content, we decided that the book would be more readable if we wrote it with one voice, so Jim has done the actual writing.

Finally, we want to acknowledge some people who have significantly contributed to what's on these pages. Don Simpson, of NavPress, has coached us along from the beginning. Glenn McMahan, Jim's son-in-law and the real writer in his family, reviewed and critiqued our work.

Over the years we have learned together with many partners in mission. John, Aldo, Ken, Rinus, Neil, Alan, Vijayan, Lynton, and Logan have helped shape our understanding in ways too numerous to mention.

Without our wives, Audrey and Marge, neither of us would have a message to share!

PART ONE:

THE
INSIDER

Part One:

INTRODUCTION

✳ ✳ ✳

I got onto the ski lift and found myself riding up the mountain with two twenty-something men from Denver. They had moved to Denver from New Jersey two years before in pursuit of employment in the tech industry. They were very fortunate, they said, to have managed to hang on to their jobs when the Nasdaq collapsed soon after they arrived.

The two had volunteered this information about themselves within the first two minutes of the ten-minute ride to the top of the mountain. It was typical ski-lift talk. "Cold today, huh? Where're you from?" According to custom, it was now my turn to talk.

"I'm from Colorado Springs—came up for the day. I'm working on a book and needed to take a break."

"Really? What's the book about?"

"The working title is, 'The Insider.' It's about making sense of life—about finding one's calling in it. I find most people don't have a clue. They put in eighty-hour weeks, going hard all the time, sometimes catching naps in their cubicles; but when you ask them where they're going in such a hurry, they give you a blank look."

I paused to read their responses. Their signal: keep talking. Because I'm old enough to ski on a senior discount ticket, I figured I could be a bit paternalistic. I kidded them, "When you came out to Denver, you probably thought you could make your bundle and retire at thirty-five. You hadn't lived long enough to know what a downturn in the market could look like. You had only seen things go up."

"Actually, we were shooting for retiring at thirty-three, but we've had to revise that," one of them joked.

"Well, whatever," I replied. "The problem of meaning really sets in the day you stop running. Are you going to be okay with spending the remaining forty years entertaining yourselves? I doubt it."

We swapped stories about people we know who have tried to do that, and agreed it doesn't work very well.

"So, where do guys like you go to get answers to questions like these? Here we are with bigotry on both sides of us: the religious fundamentalist on the right and the liberal relativist on the left. One side wants us to believe too much—while the other forbids us to believe anything at all. Where *does* one go?"

"Is that what your book is about?"

"Yeah."

"What did you say the name of it was?"

The search for meaning, in our society, is taking on a desperate edge. But, just because some of us already follow Christ doesn't mean we have it sorted out and are living purposeful lives. We can belong to Christ— and still muddle along in existential confusion. We believe eternal life awaits, but we're unable to connect the dots between that promised life and the one we're in the middle of right now. Our life can be so mundane, with such predictable daily routines—all of which roar along at frantic speed—that we find it hard to imagine anything of larger, eternal purpose actually going on.

We have observed this dilemma among people of many cultures around the world. They believe in Christ but continue to hunger for meaningful participation in God's purposes. Such participation is within reach—but many of us have yet to take hold of it. Our purpose in writing this book is to help you be successful in your search.

There are four parts to this book. In this first part, we explore the biblical foundations of our subject. We address the theology that supports *insidership*; consequently, you will find this section to be more philosophical than the other three.

Because most of our readers are practitioners and not theologians, we have worked at keeping this section readable. Our style is succinct, so you'll want to read it with care. We will be addressing some very big ideas with very few words, and they can slip past you, unobserved.

If you are a confirmed pragmatist who loves to go directly to the bottom line and are not particularly concerned about how we get there, you may want to skip this section and begin with part two. Part two addresses the obstacles that stand in the way of our fruitfulness as an insider, obstacles such as our fears and our personal limitations—things we all struggle with every day.

In part three we look at seven life patterns of a fruitful insider. Our goal is to leave the reader with a clear, doable picture of how to live as an insider.

Part four examines costs. What will it cost us individually, and as a church, to do what we've been talking about?

CHAPTER I

GOD'S ETERNAL PURPOSES AND THE INSIDER

* * *

We were just shooting the breeze, talking about whatever was on our minds, when Jack said something I will never forget. He said, "These past twenty years of my life have played out like a bad movie. As I watched them go by I kept thinking to myself, 'This wasn't the script I had in mind. It wasn't supposed to be like this.'" He paused and added, " . . . and I don't know what I can do to make the next twenty any different."

Professionally, Jack is one of the most successful people I know. He has a good marriage and children who love him. He grew up in the church as a Christian. So what was his problem?

Jack was struggling with some unfulfilled expectations. He had expected more from God than he was getting. He had expected to see God use him in his workings in the world. But here he was at the peak of his career and he could see little or nothing to indicate that God had ever done anything through him!

I know a lot of people like Jack. Many of my friends who became Christians in their college days are saying similar things. They had believed in Christ along with the news that he has "a wonderful plan for their lives"—and they could hardly wait for life to begin! But now the years have gone by—and they're still waiting!

What has gone wrong? The easiest response is to put the blame back on the person. (What can people expect when they don't make space for God in their daily lives?) Or, we could find fault with the way the gospel had been presented to them. (They believed in a hyped-up gospel that overpromised.) Or we could lay the blame on God. (He doesn't really involve himself in people's lives all that much.)

However we interpret this, Jack's problems are real. We all need to live for *something*. It's contrary to our nature to be content if we feel our lives are not counting for something that is bigger than life! God made us this way. Whatever the earthly value of our achievements, if we do not feel that what we're working on somehow transcends the here and now, we find ourselves struggling with feelings of futility. This is a universal phenomenon that runs through all of human history.

IN PURSUIT OF MEANING

THE EGYPTIAN KINGS who spent their lives—and the lives of thousands of others—building their tombs were driven by the vision of a busy, enterprising afterlife. Many of Europe's great cathedrals were substantially funded by wealthy people who exchanged their properties for promises of perpetual prayers being offered for them from the cathedrals after their deaths. They were preoccupied with their eternal status. But one does not have to be religious to have concerns of this nature. The current popularity of the idea of leaving a legacy tells us this need is common to all sorts of people. We want to give ourselves to something that will outlive us.

This was the message of Solomon, the writer of the book of

Ecclesiastes. He had both the opportunity and the means to experiment with just about every option life can offer. After doing it all he observed:

> I denied myself nothing my eyes desired;
> I refused my heart no pleasure.
> My heart took delight in all my work. . . .
> Yet when I surveyed all that my hands had done
> and what I had toiled to achieve,
> everything was meaningless, a chasing after the wind;
> nothing was gained under the sun.[1]

Solomon tried out everything "under the sun" and did not find meaning in any of it. That was his problem. His sights were too low! Our experience must extend beyond the sun to include the eternal, if we are to be satisfied. Is this need we feel not a part of our being made in God's image?

The times we spend in private devotions won't completely resolve these frustrations, either. In fact, the more we meditate on the Scriptures the stronger our desires become to know God and to participate with him in what he is doing. The Scriptures remind us again and again that following God does mean more than what Jack and my other friends are experiencing. So our question persists: What should we expect to happen in the normal course of our relationship with God?

WHAT'S IT ALL ABOUT?

NOW WE ARE asking life's biggest question. "What's this life all about? What's going on?" And there is only one place to go for the answer. It is to ask, "What is God about? What is he doing?" If we don't have it right about what he's up to, we can be sure we won't get it right in our own life.

A futile life is one lived on an agenda that has no connection with God's purposes. It doesn't matter how fast we're going, or how high we're flying, or where we're headed—if we're not living according to God's purposes, our life is futile!

What is God doing today? It's hard to tell just by looking at things. The news from around the world is consistently grim. Endemic corruption impoverishes millions of people in country after country. Tribal wars turn millions more into refugees. Diseases of epidemic proportions are killing millions a year in Africa alone. As I write this, the news from India reports a massive earthquake with a death toll of over fifteen thousand people. The same newscast informs us of a famine in central Asia where thousands are dying of starvation.

But we aren't going to hear much more on these horror stories. There isn't room on the news hour for such incidentals. The newscasters need the time to cover "The War on Terror" and the other major conflicts going on around the world!

To suggest that in the midst of this agonizing chaos God has purposes and that he is actively pursuing them is quite a stretch! It is easier to believe that things are falling apart and that he is absent from the scene. The Scriptures, however, tell us the opposite! They tell us God is at work, bringing all things together.

The Eternal Purposes of God

IT WAS ABOUT A.D. 60 when the apostle Paul wrote his letter to the emerging community of believers in Ephesus. Ephesus was also famous as the center of the worship of Cybele/Artemis, a goddess of fertility. Her temple was regarded as one of the Seven Wonders of the World. Sorcery, occult practices, and prostitution were a part of the worship practices of the temple. The new believers Paul was writing to were picking their way out of all of this. Life in the church was still pretty ragged.

Yet look at how Paul opens his letter. He addresses it to "the saints in Ephesus, the faithful in Christ Jesus."[2] He is reminding them of who they are! They have a dual citizenship. They are "in Ephesus" but they are also "in Christ." Yes, they belong to Christ, but they are to live out this new life within the realities of the city of Ephesus.

Paul wants the Ephesian believers to understand that despite all that is going on around them, they are a part of and are significant to God's eternal purposes. With a few words he paints the cosmic landscape. He writes:

> He chose us in him before the creation of the world . . . to be adopted as his sons through Jesus Christ. . . . In him we have redemption through his blood, the forgiveness of sins. . . . He made known to us the mystery of his will . . . which he purposed in Christ . . . to bring all things in heaven and on earth together under one head, even Christ.[3]

This paragraph is filled with vital information. God has purposes. He has a plan and right now he is in the midst of working it out. This is not an emergency rescue operation that God is performing, a sort of "plan B" after things went wrong. This plan was in place before God created anything at all! We also learn that at the center of this plan is the creation of a people, and that the cost of getting them would be the blood of his Son. In summary, this passage tells us that life has to do with a *people* and a *cross*!

This same idea is addressed in Psalm 2. It opens describing a revolution in progress—the human powers revolting against God. "The kings of the earth take their stand and the rulers gather together against the LORD and against his Anointed One." Down with God! Up with us! We don't need him! they chant. "'Let us break their chains,' they say, 'and throw off their fetters.'" We're taking over!

The demonstration is interrupted by laughter. Someone is laughing! It's God! "The One enthroned in heaven laughs; the Lord scoffs at them." This rebellion is so ludicrous it makes God laugh! He addresses the rebels: Look over there. Look at the throne you intended to occupy. It's already filled. My Son is on it! "I have installed my King on Zion, my holy hill." Then God turns to his Son and says, "You are my Son. . . . Ask of me." What can I give you for your inheritance? The Father offers, "I will make the nations your inheritance, the ends of the earth your possession."

Here again, we come away with the same message. Attempting to live apart from God is foolish, even if you're a king. What is God doing? He is creating an inheritance for his Son. It consists of *people* of all nations.

THE DAY OF THE REFUGEE

BUT, NOW, WHAT is this next statement God makes to his Son? He says, "You will rule them with an iron scepter; you will dash them to pieces like pottery." What is he talking about? Who is going to be dashed to pieces? It's the rebel kings, those who were revolting against God! He tells them, "You kings . . . be warned, you rulers of the earth . . . Kiss the son, lest he be angry and you be destroyed."[4]

Throughout history, ever since these words were written, God has repeatedly acted on this promise to his Son. A society builds a system that, in time, shuts God out. As the rebellion of its leaders hardens, the people in that society are deprived of any direct news about God. At some point, God intervenes. Suddenly, the repressive system is no more!

This is, indeed, what is happening all around the world today. God is breaking to pieces the powers that rule people's lives, the things they believe in, the things they have traditionally looked to for security. Governments, economies, cultures, markets, and religious systems occupying people's minds and souls for centuries are breaking apart. The "isms" are falling and the people these systems held captive are being freed to become part of Christ's inheritance. The refugee is a good example.

I have a friend, Isma'il, who is living as a refugee in a Middle Eastern country. His home country is Iraq, but he and hundreds of thousands of other Iraqis have migrated to this particular country in search of a more secure place to live. Isma'il is a contagious follower of Christ, living in the midst of a solidly Muslim society. Over the past two years he, with the help of a few friends, has planted the gospel in five different communities of refugees, where it is now taking root and growing. The uncertainties of life for the refugee combined with the newfound space to think and seek truth are breaking up the hold of the Muslim religion and creating fertile ground for the good news of Christ. This is happening in many places around the world.

It's All Coming Together

GOD IS BRINGING "all things in heaven and on earth together under one head, even Christ."[5] This phrase, "bring . . . together," is the verb *anakephalaioo*. It expresses the idea of gathering things together to present them as a whole. In rhetoric, the word is used to describe summing up the argument and to show how each part of it fits together to substantiate the thesis. In math, the verb refers to the process of adding up columns of figures and then putting the sum at the top. All of the pieces that make up this chaotic world will be put in their places, and the picture will become clear!

So God continues to create! Jesus said, "My Father is always at his work to this very day, and I, too, am working."[6] This time he is creating an eternal people who will be his citizens, his heirs, his household, and his family.

This outcome is not in doubt. Coming out of a vision, the apostle John reported what he had seen:

> I looked and there before me was a great multitude that no one
> could count, from every nation, tribe, people and language,
> standing before the throne and in front of the Lamb. . . . They
> cried out in a loud voice:

> "Salvation belongs to our God,
> who sits on the throne,
> and to the Lamb."[7]

There they are! It's as good as done. God is bringing his eternal family together. Today, God looks at this same chaos we fret over and says, It's all coming together! In spite of the mess mankind is making, my work is right on schedule.

A People and a Cross — and Jack

SO WHAT ABOUT Jack? God is working in this world, but Jack doesn't feel he has a part in that work. It has turned out that the main feature in most Christians' lives today is congregating. This makes most of us passive participants. Jack is not comfortable with that. His problem is, he too lives in an Ephesus. He knows in his heart that he has an inside track on a world of lost people — and he doesn't know what to do with that! Most of his waking hours are spent rubbing shoulders with people who are in one self-destruct mode or another. But he feels like an alien in their midst. He lives a divided life. One part of it is in church; the other is in society. He senses there has to be a way to bring these two worlds together to where all the parts of his life — his work, social life, leisure, and civic activities—count for something.

Jack probably couldn't put this into words, but he realizes something big is missing! He isn't interested in adding another activity to his life. He's already too busy. He isn't looking for an evangelistic program that will help him reach some of his friends. Programs begin and end. He's looking for something bigger than that. Jack needs to engage his life with God's purposes in ways that endure. He longs to live all of life to the glory of God!

That's why we've written this book. We want to help people like Jack understand their calling to participate in what God is doing today. We want people to see that this calling is to be worked out within their existing relational networks where they are already positioned as *insiders*. God intends that every part of our daily life should line up with his purposes, to his glory. We believe this is something that is within reach for all of us, not just the gifted few.

THE CALL TO THE KINGDOM OF GOD

* * *

God is at work, creating. Some of us thought he was done with that sort of thing when he announced that he had finished this creation. When he finished, didn't he declare a Sabbath, and didn't he rest? He rested from that work, but apparently he has another creation going on right now! What is he doing? We only have fragments of the picture, but he has revealed enough of it for us to get the idea. He is creating a people, an eternal people! He is gathering them out of every nation and from every generation—to present them to his Son as "a bride beautifully dressed for her husband."[1] What an astonishing metaphor for an even more astonishing work!

Other metaphors used to describe this people he is creating are equally revealing. They are called Christ's "inheritance," "citizens," "members of God's household," and "a dwelling in which God lives."[2] All of these descriptions suggest intimacy of relationship. Is God saying he is creating a people who will be at his table as full family members? Does he actually intend for them to reign with him? That's what it sounds like. He is creating an eternal people!

If that is what God is doing, if in these days he is creating such a people, should we not expect to see signs of this activity all around us, every day? But where are these signs? What should we be looking for? Strategies for global evangelization? Massive movements of people entering our churches? Not necessarily! We would probably miss it if we looked for them in these directions. We need to train our eyes to see the kingdom of God.

THE KINGDOM OF GOD—WHAT IS IT?

ANYONE WHO HAS read much of the Bible is familiar with the term "the kingdom of God." Most of us, however, slip past it without much thought. We imagine the kingdom as something that will happen someday, off in the future. We know God will, eventually, set all things right. But, we think, today is today, and we're running late. There isn't the time to get philosophical right now! So, we fail to see the kingdom of God, which is all around us, and we miss the countless opportunities daily life presents us with to live like the kingdom citizen we are—if Christ, indeed, is in us. "He has rescued us from the dominion of darkness and brought us [past tense] into the kingdom of the Son he loves."[3] In a sense, we are already there. The kingdom has come. It is in us as we go about our affairs *today*. We need to understand this truth if we, as insiders, are to fruitfully participate in this work God is doing.

The kingdom runs like a thread throughout the Bible, from Genesis to Revelation. As the Old Testament unfolds, we progressively learn more about the scope of God's realm and the nature of his reign. The narrative begins with the Creator, God, delegating the rulership of the natural world and all its creatures to mankind. To this day, we carry this responsibility, by his authority.

Moses experienced God's rule when he found himself on the safe side of the Red Sea, together with all the people of Israel, and saw Pharaoh's army washed up on shore, dead. To mark the occasion, Moses wrote a song that ends with the words, "The LORD will reign forever and ever."[4] The eternal nature of God's rule is a theme repeated over and over throughout the Bible.

The psalmists carry the description of the kingdom further. Psalm 97 begins with the words, "The LORD reigns, let the earth be glad; let the distant shores rejoice. . . . Righteousness and justice are the foundation of his throne."[5] This phrase "righteousness and justice" is frequently used in the Scriptures to describe the kingdom of God. You can count on it. God's rule is always just, and it is always according to what is true. This is both frightening and reassuring. Justice exists!

Nebuchadnezzar, a pagan king who ruled Babylon around 600 B.C., had the good fortune of learning this lesson before it was too late. And in the course of his lesson he became an unlikely contributor to our further understanding of the kingdom. To get his attention and to humble him, God took him through a strange experience in which he lived as a madman for seven years. When he returned to his senses he gave one of the clearest descriptions of the kingdom we find in Scripture. He said,

His dominion is an eternal dominion;
his kingdom endures from generation to generation.
All the peoples of the earth
are regarded as nothing.
He does as he pleases
with the powers of heaven
and the peoples of the earth.
No one can hold back his hand
or say to him: "What have you done?"[6]

Nebuchadnezzar understood the nature of God's kingdom—that there never was a time when it did not exist; that it always was, that it is, and that it always will be.

Given the sweep of this theme throughout the Old Testament, it should have been no surprise to us that the kingdom was a central theme of Jesus' teachings. At the very beginning of his ministry, Matthew records, "From that time on Jesus began to preach, 'Repent, for the kingdom of heaven is near.'"[7] Matthew refers to the kingdom about fifty times in his gospel, and the other evangelists follow suit.

Nevertheless, nobody in Jesus' day seemed to understand much of what he was talking about. People heard his words, looked around, but couldn't see anything that looked to them like a kingdom. But the Scriptures indicate it had, indeed, come! It was there, among them.

The very last question the apostles asked Jesus just before he ascended into heaven is a good example of this confusion. They asked, "Lord, are you at this time going to restore the kingdom to Israel?"[8] They still couldn't see the kingdom because they were looking for the wrong thing. Because they were looking for a physical system, a political solution to the social mess they were in, they missed the kingdom entirely. They missed it even though Jesus explained, "The kingdom of God does not come with your careful observation, nor will people say, 'Here it is,' or, 'There it is,' because the kingdom of God is within you."[9] I suggest that, today, we still miss seeing it—for the same reason. We look for the kingdom in the wrong places.

According to Jesus, the kingdom of God is within certain *people*. It is not in our structures, nor in our organizations, nor in our sweeping strategies for world evangelization that we will see the kingdom. We observe it by watching its citizens, who are among us like seeds sown in a field, seeds that have fallen into the ground, are dying, and generating new life; who are like salt on a plate of food flavoring the whole; or like a lighted window on a darkened hillside giving a point of reference to everyone around them. We see the kingdom by observing how certain people live their lives!

In our culture, an unheralded individual is about the last place we'd ever think of looking to find anything of importance. We live in a world where "good" is defined by size, where "big" is good, and bigger is better. We measure the success of anything, whether it's a business or a church, by its volume, by the amount we amass of whatever it is we're working at, whether it's money or people. In our value system, we don't begin to pay attention to people until there are lots of them in one place together. We count them to decide whether or not what is happening is important. We neglect to stop and look at the life next to us. So, we miss the kingdom—even though it's right there in front of us!

Elijah, a powerful prophet, missed it too. He was really down. He had just faced off with King Ahab and his four hundred prophets of Baal, and he was exhausted. He had lost his perspective and just wanted to die. So God attended to him. God told him, Go to that mountain over there and I will visit you. Elijah went, probably scared, and wondering what it would be like, this personal visit from God. First, there came a rock-shattering wind. Next came an earthquake, and then a fire. Each time Elijah must have thought, *This is it! This has got to be him!* But it wasn't. Finally, after all the fireworks, there came a gentle whisper—and that was God, speaking to him! A soft voice. This was a prelude to the way the great King himself arrived seven hundred years later.[10]

HOW TO RECOGNIZE THE KINGDOM WHEN YOU SEE IT

JESUS TOLD A parable in Matthew 25 that helps us understand what to look for when watching for the kingdom.

In the story, the Son of Man is on his throne with all the peoples of the earth gathered before him. He divides them into two groups. He invites those in one group to take their inheritance—places in the kingdom he had been preparing for them. The other group is sent into judgment. He explained the difference. He said, These served me when I was hungry, thirsty, needing a place to stay, needing clothes, feeling sick, and when I was in jail, but the others did not.

None of the guests, however, could remember this king ever being in jail or suffering needs of any sort, nor could they recall ever doing any of those things for him. So they asked him, When did we do that for you? He replied, "Whatever you did for one of the least of these brothers of mine, you did for me."[11] We see the kingdom whenever we see people acting "kingdomly"; whenever, because of their love for God, they love the people in their lives.

Once we learn how to watch for the kingdom of God we can see it everywhere. We can see it every day, in the affairs of the people around us.

A friend of mine has a business that needed to be restructured if it was to have a future. He had to downsize his staff by half, something he hated to do. But he did it, clumsily. People were hurt and got angry. Instead of just putting it all behind him and moving on, he reached out to each one by acknowledging the wrong he had done and communicating his awareness of their hurt. He did this because he wants to run his business according to the ways of Christ.

A woman went through a divorce and found herself alone and responsible to raise her infant child. She had to give up her business to care for the child. Losses such as this are a recipe for resentment and anger. Instead, two years later, her life communicates joy and thankfulness to God. In her pain, she turned to him rather than resorting to her own wits to put the broken pieces together.

Another friend is recovering from a double mastectomy, months of chemotherapy, and weeks of radiation. She got beyond the fear and pain and spent the year interceding for her children and others. Rather than blaming God and indulging in self-pity, she bore beautiful fruit in other people's lives even while desperately ill. Her hope in the unshakable sustains her.

I am married to a person who lives tuned-in to the needs of others. She often spots them before they are even aware they have the need. She fits the wedding dress for her friend's daughter, fixes a meal for a sick neighbor, handles the stateside banking for a missionary family, and on and on. She serves because that's the way Christ lived his life.

Many people must downsize their companies; we all know people who go through divorces and end up as single moms; hundreds get cancer every day. People with needs surround us. We are so accustomed to seeing such things that we accept as normal the resentment, anger, and absorption with self that usually characterize people's responses. But we know the kingdom is among us whenever we see people, motivated by Christ's rule in their hearts, showing mercy instead of judgment, speaking the truth instead of spinning it, giving grace instead of seeking revenge, serving people instead of using them.

When we see things such as these happening, we know that God's rule is established. For now, it is in people's hearts and we see only its signs. These "sightings" are previews of the day when "every knee should bow . . . and every tongue confess that Jesus Christ is Lord."[12] Many will bow in defeat, others in celebration!

THE COMMUNITY OF THE KINGDOM

THE WITNESS OF a single life lived under Christ's rule is powerful. But the skeptic will discount it. He or she will explain it away as being a mutation: "She was born a caring person. That can happen." But as kingdom citizens live their lives together, actually loving one another, it becomes a different matter. Such a community—whether it is a family, a few believ-ers in a neighborhood, a network of business people, or a church con-gregation—makes a persuasive statement to an onlooking world that the kingdom, indeed, is among them. The message of the kingdom is amplified as its citizens live out their unique calling in community. As they do, the kingdom grows.

In his book *The Rise of Christianity*, Rodney Stark explores the fasci-nating question "How did a tiny and obscure messianic movement from the edge of the Roman empire dislodge classical paganism and become the dominant faith of Western civilization in a few centuries?"[13] The explanation that came out of his research was essentially that expan-sion resulted from the Christians' belief that God loved them. "If," they reasoned, "God loves humanity, Christians may not please God unless they 'love one another.'"[14] Given the moral climate of the day in the Roman Empire, this was revolutionary stuff. Educated pagans would have dismissed the notion that the gods care how we treat one another. They would have found that absurd. Classical philosophers of the day "regarded mercy and pity as pathological emotions—defects of character to be avoided by all rational men." Because mercy involves providing unearned help or relief, it was contrary to justice. Pity was "a defect of character unworthy of the wise and excusable only in those who have not yet grown up."[15]

The Roman world was groaning under every sort of misery, filled with capricious cruelties and a love of violent death. As Christians acted out in daily life the command not just to love one another but also those beyond the boundaries of family, Christian community, and tribe, they provided the cultural basis for a revitalization of the Roman world. Christians taught their converts to be humane, to live not according to the culture of the empire but according to God's rule in their hearts. The ways of God's kingdom ruled them.

THE KINGDOM OF GOD AND THE INSIDER

JESUS SUMMARIZED HIS life's ministry with the words, "I have brought you glory on earth by completing the work you gave me to do."[16] Jesus was here to reveal, to everyone who saw him, what his Father was like. That's what it means to *glorify*. It is to reflect God and his ways. We, too, glorify God by doing our work according to his rule in our heart. It is in the little things more than in the big things that this happens, that God and his kingdom are revealed. Anyone can be good on stage. It is in the attitudes and reactions, in the things that happen too fast for thought, in that flash of anger or of pride that the real person is seen. When our reactions reveal grace and truth, we are acting out of character with our sinful nature, but in character with our kingdom citizenship.

By our standards, the ways of the kingdom seem so weak, so insignificant, so unworthy of the bother. The kingdom is in the small voice, in the unobtrusive act. Yet it cannot be shaken! We cannot market it, yet it advances forcibly. We cannot build it; we can only receive it. It is subversive against the systems of our society because it turns values upside down. It is the way of life of the *insider*.

Living out one's kingdom citizenship here and now is foundational to one's fruitfulness as an insider. That is because we are sowing seed by giving glimpses of the ways of the kingdom to the people in our traffic patterns. We are serving notice to them that the eternal has, indeed, invaded the present!

CHAPTER 3

A VISION FOR SPIRITUAL GENERATIONS

"The least of you will become a thousand,
the smallest a mighty nation.
I am the LORD;
in its time I will do this swiftly."

(ISAIAH 60:22)

✻ ✻ ✻

I f we are not looking in the right places to see the kingdom of God, we will probably not be focusing our efforts on the right things either. What should we be giving ourselves to?

I was introduced to the idea of spiritual generations in the early days of my walk with Christ. It's the idea of an individual who, when he multiplies, becomes a multitude through a sort of spiritual geometric progression. There was a story going around at the time that communicated the idea.

A simple citizen of India did something that pleased the king. To compensate, the king offered to grant him one wish. In response, the citizen asked to have a checkerboard brought to him. He asked the king to place

37

one grain of wheat on the first square, double it to two on the second square, double it again to four on the third, and so on until he had repeated the process on all sixty-four squares. A foolish wish, when he could have had anything he wanted, thought the king—until he tried to meet the request. The volume of wheat involved, so the story goes, would cover India with fifty feet of wheat. I wasn't sure who did the math on this story, but even so, give or take a foot or two of wheat, I got the point.

Another illustration I heard at about the same time added fuel to the idea. In this one, we begin with only one Christian in the world. He shares Christ with a friend, and there are two. They spend a year together growing in Christ. Then they each repeat the process with another friend. There are now four. After another year each of the four reaches one more, and so on. In thirty-four years the total would be more than the population of the world!

This was heady stuff and it captured my imagination. The idea of spiritual multiplication showed how an ordinary person could have a global influence in the course of living an ordinary life. I liked that and set out to pursue it as a part of my life's vision. Second Timothy 2:2 was my proof text, where Paul instructed Timothy, "The things you have heard me say . . . entrust to reliable men who will also be qualified to teach others." Here were four generations: Paul, Timothy, reliable men, and on to others! I didn't stop to consider that Paul was instructing Timothy in how to develop the leaders the young movement would need. He wasn't giving him a strategy for discipling the nations!

It didn't take long, after embarking on this pursuit of spiritual generations, to realize that there was something wrong with my thinking. I couldn't make the idea work in real life. As I wondered about this I understood why. I was pursuing a vision based on a few illustrations and logic rather than on biblical truth.

So I went to the Bible. What does it say about spiritual generations?

I asked. Does it say anything at all? I found the biblical picture to be far more compelling than the illustrations. Those had served to awaken me to an important idea, but had also put me on a wrong track in both my approach and in my expectations.

WHAT DO THE SCRIPTURES SAY?

THE BIBLE IS the account of God searching for and reaching out to people who, because of their rebellion, have lost their way and are heading toward judgment. He is reaching out to all peoples of all nations, and of all generations. There is a consistent pattern to the way he carries out this work that repeats itself from one end of Scripture to the other.

The Bible uses just eleven chapters to tell the story of God's creation of the world, of mankind, of their fall into sin, and of the formation of the nations. These are eleven amazingly full chapters! Then, Genesis 12 opens with God seeking out a man and giving him specific instructions on what he is to do. Along with those instructions, God gave this man a startling promise. He said, "I will make you into a great nation . . . and all peoples on earth will be blessed through you."[1] What an improbable statement! How could all the peoples of the earth benefit from this person's life?

The person God chose was Abram, who would become Abraham, the "father of many nations."[2] God looked beyond Abraham across all the generations of the future to the day when he would fulfill his purposes for all mankind through keeping that promise! This promise to Abraham marked the start of something new. From that point on the biblical story builds on this promise, right down to its end.

On another day God came to Abraham's son, Isaac, and said, "I will be with you and will bless you . . . [I] will confirm the oath I swore to your father Abraham . . . and through your offspring all nations on earth will be blessed."[3] Here God added another piece to the emerging picture.

The fulfillment of God's promise to the nations would begin with Isaac's physical generations. The blessing on the nations will come through his children.

Isaac's son Jacob had a similar experience. God also appeared to him with a message. He told him, "Your descendants will be like the dust of the earth. . . . All peoples on earth will be blessed through you and your offspring."[4] Jacob had twelve sons, and the nation began to take form.

We pick the story up again several hundred years later. At this point, almost seven hundred years had passed since God told Abraham to leave his homeland in pursuit of the promise. Abraham's children were by then known as *Israelites,* and they numbered over a million. Life had not been easy. They had spent 430 of those years as slaves, and then another forty wandering in the desert. But, finally, they are entering the land God had promised their fathers years before. The slavery in Egypt and the desert wandering had been their school, to prepare them for what God was bringing them into. Now Moses, their leader, gives them a final pre-entry summary on how to live in this land once they take possession of it.

At the heart of these instructions we again find this same pattern in God's workings. He continues to look into the future at the nations of the world, down through the corridor of Israel's generations yet to be born. He tells the people to obey his commands "so that you, your children and their children after them may fear the LORD your God as long as you live . . . so that you may enjoy long life . . . so that it may go well with you."[5] God was concerned for their well-being. He knows life goes better for people who live by his laws.

But there was another reason why this obedience was so important. It was not just for Israel's good; it was that he had his eye on all the nations of the world. He intended that the Israelites, by the way they lived, would reveal who he is and what he is like to all their neighbors. Referring to the laws God had given them, Moses says, "Observe them carefully, for this will show your wisdom and understanding to the nations, who will hear about all these decrees and say, 'Surely this great nation is a wise and understanding people.' What other nation is so great as to have their gods near them the way the Lord our God is near us?"[6]

Now we begin to understand that the momentum of this spreading of the news about God was to build from generation to generation. The psalmist wrote,

> I will open my mouth in parables,
> I will utter hidden things, things from of old—
> what we have heard and known,
> what our fathers have told us.
> We will not hide them from their children;
> we will tell the next generation
> the praiseworthy deeds of the Lord . . .
> which he commanded our forefathers
> to teach their children,
> so the next generation would know them,
> even the children yet to be born,
> and they in turn would tell their children.[7]

As this story continues to unfold we will see that God's purpose was to reveal himself to the peoples of the world through a combination of both physical and spiritual generations, beginning with Israel. The accumulated spiritual heritage that he had given Israel, as it was passed from parents to children, would gather momentum and become an undeniable statement about himself to their neighbors and, ultimately, to the nations of the world. The nations would see, understand, and acknowledge him as God.

KING DAVID—HIS HERITAGE AND HIS LEGACY

KING DAVID'S PERSONAL history is an illustration of the power of this spiritual heritage as it is passed on from one generation to the next. In the time when judges led Israel, an Israelite woman was widowed while living in Moab; her name was Naomi. Her two sons, both of whom had married women from Moab, also died soon after their father did. Destitute, Naomi decided to return to her own people and encouraged her two daughters-in-law to return to theirs. One of the wives, Ruth, insisted on staying with Naomi, so together they traveled back to Naomi's hometown of Bethlehem. We are all familiar with Ruth's explanation for her decision. We occasionally hear it at weddings. She said, "Where you go I will go, and where you stay I will stay. Your people will be my people and your God my God."[8]

There in Bethlehem, Ruth married Boaz, a man of impeccable character. They named their son Obed. He was the father of Jesse, who was David's father. It took three generations of godly living to lay the foundations upon which David lived his life. Thus, he had a head start in the formation of his faith and character. He would need it!

Like Abraham, David was given a promise that is pivotal to God's dealings with all mankind. God told him, "I took you from the pasture and from following the flock to be ruler over my people Israel. . . . I will raise up your offspring to succeed you. . . . I will establish the throne of his kingdom forever. . . . Your throne will be established forever."[9]

What an unimaginable thing to say to a person! No kingdom can last forever! Where are the Babylonian, Greek, Roman, Mayan, Aztec, Iberian, British, and all the other empires? Our past and present kingdoms vanish, some literally from one day to the next. But David's still stands! What sort of kingdom might this be?

Isaiah clears up this question. He prophesied, "A shoot will come up from the stump of Jesse; from his roots a Branch will bear fruit."[10] Jesse, David's father, is a forefather to the promised Messiah. So David's throne is eternal in that the eternal king, Jesus Christ, came to us through that lineage. David prefigured the Messiah. These promises and prophecies concerning David's throne are really about the Messiah, Jesus Christ. He is the new, eternal David.

The apostle Peter made this clear in his first public sermon. He told of how Jesus' resurrection fulfilled prophecies made about David. David, said Peter, prophesied that his body would not decay in a grave and that he would ascend into heaven where he would be seated at the Father's right hand.[11] That statement had to sound like a riddle to the listeners. Everybody in the audience knew where David's body was buried! Of course it had decomposed over the centuries it had lain there. That was Peter's point. So, he continued, David could not have been talking about himself! David died, but his throne is still occupied; it is occupied by Jesus the Messiah!

God used this avenue of generations to bring us his Son. He thereby created a context in which his coming would be anticipated by many and could be understood by all. It provides for us today one more of those infallible proofs that Jesus was who he claimed to be.

JESUS FULFILLS THE PROMISES

GOD DID NOT drop what he was doing with Abraham to move on to something else once his Son came into the picture. Jesus didn't change the story—he wrote its last chapter. He is the fulfillment of God's promises to Abraham. Paul explains, "The promises were spoken to Abraham and to his seed. The Scripture does not say 'and to seeds,' meaning many people, but 'and to your seed,' meaning one person, who is Christ."[12] Now it really gets amazing! Paul adds, "Understand, then, that those who believe are children of Abraham."[13] And again, "If you belong to Christ, then you are Abraham's seed, and heirs according to the promise."[14] Am I, a person of English-Danish descent, born in a small town in Minnesota, a child of Abraham? Yes, that's what it means!

It now becomes apparent that God never was thinking merely about physical generations in his instructions to Israel. He intended a convergence of physical generations with the spiritual, right from the beginning. God had this generation of ours in mind when he gave Abraham his promise. We, too, are children of Abraham and, as such, have rights to those same promises! This truth is borne out by the things Jesus taught and did.

SEED, SEEDS, AND MORE SEED

IT WAS NOT coincidental that Jesus constantly used agricultural stories and metaphors to get his message across. He told stories about vineyards, fields, different kinds of soil, and about sowing seed. He spoke of laborers working in the fields and about the mystery of a dying seed giving birth to new life. True, he was talking to an agrarian society, but it was more that that. He was explaining how things pertaining to the kingdom of God actually work in this world. The stories describe the ways of the kingdom as it grows among us. It is consistent with everything else we have seen so far about God's workings as he reaches out to this wayward world. Again, it is the small, the insignificant, the unobtrusive bearing of fruit right alongside the "sons of the evil one."[15]

GENERATIONS AND JESUS

IMAGINE THE CHALLENGE of the task Jesus faced! He came to be the Lamb of God. To accomplish this he had to live a life that revealed the

Father to everyone who saw him; die as God's sacrifice for every sin that has ever been and ever will be committed; defeat death; and then—when that was finished—return to the Father. It was also essential that he do all this in such a way that every generation from his until ours, and beyond, would have the news of it. His sacrifice would have been in vain if the message of it ever died out along the way.

How would you have tackled this challenge in communication? Jesus began by inviting a few people to follow him. Together they went from town to town where he attracted multitudes through his miracles and his teaching. Occasionally, he would invite one or another to travel along with him. People didn't know what to make of him. Controversy over his identity arose everywhere he went.

As the crowds thickened, the motives of some of the people who followed him got mixed up. They could take him as a prophet, a teacher, or even as their king. But they couldn't handle the idea that he was the eternal God. So, to keep them from deluding themselves further, Jesus gave them more truth than they could handle, which sent most of them on their way. Upset with his teaching, they quit following him. Clearly, the few survivors—a little handful of ordinary, unedu-cated people—were his priority.[16] Time was precious, and running out. He had only three or four years to get everything done. Yet, day after day, he gave those few people his full attention. He was growing seed for the future.

SEED FOR THE FUTURE

JUST BEFORE JESUS was arrested he spent time in prayer with his Father. In that prayer, which is recorded in John 17, Jesus reviewed the work he had done in his years of public ministry. In it we see why he did what he did, and what he had in mind all along.

Apparently, the Father had given his Son a task to accomplish. Jesus told him, "I have brought you glory on earth by completing the work you gave me to do."[17] What was that work? He goes on to explain, "I have revealed you to those whom you gave me out of the world. They were yours; you gave them to me and they have obeyed your word."[18] Who was Jesus talking about? We find out in verse 12, as Jesus continues, "None has been lost except the one doomed to destruction," referring to Judas, who betrayed him. Jesus was praying for the twelve men he was preparing to send into all the world as apostles or "sent ones."

In this prayer, Jesus also revealed what he had in mind for those men in the future. He said,

> "I will remain in the world no longer, but they are still in the world. . . . My prayer is not that you take them out of the world but that you protect them from the evil one. . . . As you sent me into the world, I have sent them into the world. . . . My prayer is not for them alone. I pray also for those who will believe in me through their message . . . so that the world may believe that you have sent me."[19]

They were his replacements!

Here, once again, we have the same, by now familiar, pattern. What began with Jesus Christ was comprehended by a few. The few went to the nations, "teaching them to obey everything" Jesus had taught them.[20] They repeated with others what he had done with them. Obviously, they couldn't get to everyone. But those who did receive their message became, in turn, messengers themselves. Thus, God's promises to Abraham and to David continue to be fulfilled around the world to this day.

We too are a part of this genealogy of spiritual generations. He has sown us in the world as spiritual seed.

How Did It Go?

THE ACCOUNT OF the first days of the early church in the first chapters of Acts gives a very different picture from the one I've been describing. It reads more like an explosion than the gradual progress of agricultural growth.

The story begins with 120 people in a room waiting, praying, talking. These were the core people of Jesus' ministry. It was Pentecost in Jerusalem, so the city was filled with "God-fearing Jews from every nation under heaven."[21]

When the Holy Spirit arrived to indwell these people, as Jesus had promised he would, he signaled his arrival by empowering them with the ability to speak the native languages of the religious pilgrims who had filled the city. As the crowd gathered around in wonder, Peter stood up and explained from the Scriptures what was going on. As a result, about three thousand people believed and were baptized on that day. This was just the beginning!

The ranks of the church continued to swell over the next weeks and months as the apostles boldly explained what was happening and as they healed many with great displays of God's power. Luke reports that "the Lord added to their number daily those who were being saved."[22]

The city fathers tried to shut the whole thing down. They threatened, then arrested, and then imprisoned the apostles, but the ranks of God's people continued to swell. Believers gathered daily in Solomon's Colonnade and ate together in their homes. They also managed to retain the respect of the citizens of Jerusalem. As a result, "more and more men and women believed in the Lord and were added to their number."[23] Even the opposition admitted, "You have filled Jerusalem with your teaching."[24]

What was it we were saying about small, insignificant beginnings? This reads more like the start-up of a megachurch! How do we reconcile the two scenarios? Consider the raw material that went into this first church. It was made up of devout Jews and proselytes—people who were on a religious pilgrimage. This was harvest time! It was harvest time for a crop that had been almost two thousand years in the ripening—from the time of Abraham to Jesus himself. Undoubtedly, many had personally seen and heard him when he and his disciples had visited their villages. He had surely healed some of them!

On one occasion Jesus told his disciples, "I sent you to reap what you have not worked for. Others have done the hard work, and you have reaped the benefits of their labor."[25] They were to reap what the patriarchs and the prophets had sown. Once the gospel began to spread out beyond those who were so especially prepared, the pace of growth slowed dramatically. Often we fail to understand this!

I've watched people who seem to spend their lives attempting to reproduce the results of the first chapters of the book of Acts. When they fail, they think something is wrong either with themselves or with someone else. Even the apostle Paul never saw a duplication of that first response in Jerusalem! When we examine the results of Paul's ministry carefully, we observe that he usually left a small foundation of people consisting of a few households. Sometimes, very few!

We like to think there are shortcuts to taking the gospel to the nations of the world. As a society of entrepreneurs it's hard for us to accept the idea that shortcuts might not exist. We believe that if we can just plan a little bigger and can give enough money we can make it happen. But it doesn't work that way. Occasionally we hear reports of large numbers responding somewhere in the world. But, sometimes, when we investigate these reports we find there is little or nothing that endured by way of fruit. The rule seems to stand, with few exceptions: Where there has been little sowing there will be little reaping.

Rodney Stark, whom we referred to in the previous chapter, makes a fascinating contribution to this discussion. Stark, a sociologist, researched the question of the church's growth over the first three centuries with the tools of his profession. He applied the methods and models used in the social sciences to the historical materials and data we have on those first centuries of growth.[26]

He estimates that the total number of believers at the end of the first century didn't exceed 7,530. That was a mere 0.0126 percent of the population! According to him, growth was steady over those first three centuries, at about 43 percent a decade. That's about 3.1 percent annually. Such a growth rate, if sustained, would have been sufficient to position Christianity as the predominant religion in the empire when Constantine came onto the scene in A.D. 317. There is no evidence in the history of the first three centuries of the church, he says, of a sudden, massive influx of new believers. He observes that "Christianity did not grow because of miracle working in the marketplaces . . . it grew because Christians constituted an intense community. . . . The primary means of its growth was through the united and motivated efforts of the growing numbers of Christian believers, who invited their friends, relatives and neighbors to share the 'good news'."[27] "Conversion," he maintains, "was a network phenomenon based on interpersonal attachments."[28] They somehow managed to live as community and, at the same time, retain relationships with society. They did not become a ghetto unto themselves.

DOES THIS ACTUALLY WORK?

DALBY WAS A second-year student at the Universidade de Parana in Curitiba, Brazil, when I first met him. Fresh from a small, rural town in the western part of the state of Parana, he needed all the help he could get to find his way into life as a new student in a big city. It was 1967. Ken Lottis, my partner in a ministry the two of us, along with our wives, were starting up among university students, encountered Dalby and befriended him. As their friendship grew, Dalby joined a little Bible study Ken had put together. It took him about a year to decide to follow Jesus Christ.

Life had not been kind to Dalby. As he began to grow in his faith, he had to sort through the hurts and habits that were complicating everything he tried to do. But with the help of the Holy Spirit, Ken, and a small cell of other new believers like himself, the Scriptures began to shape his life.

Dalby had a desire to share his faith from the beginning. He was back in his hometown a few months after his new birth, with the desire to pass the news on to his brothers and sisters. Looking for a bit of spiritual fellowship, he visited the local priest. After a few hours of conversation and a bottle of wine, the priest said, "You really believe all this, don't you?" Dalby replied, "Yes, of course. Don't you?" The priest admitted that he didn't, that he was where he was because of the influence and authority the position gave him in the community.

The next time Dalby went home, he visited the priest again. This time, the priest proudly showed him a new Bible he had just purchased! They began to read it together, just as Ken had done with Dalby. This went on for months with sessions extending from three to six hours in length. This was Dalby's first experience in sharing his faith.

Dalby graduated from the university with a degree in architecture, married Jane, and together they set out to make their way through life. Years have passed since then.

Four months ago, my wife, Marge, and I had dinner with Dalby and Jane. It was a generation later! Their four daughters are now at about the age Dalby was when we first met. We were struck by what we saw. Here was a couple who had followed God through thick and thin. The fire was still there, only stronger!

Running a business in an economy with an inflation rate of up to 40 percent per month is like trying to fill a tub that has no stopper with water. They had succeeded at this—but just barely.

Dalby and Jane are currently living in a small town of German immigrants because he found work as an architect there. When they move on, they will leave behind a nucleus of new believers. They also have spiritual offspring scattered in several other places in the country. They are good seed.

The most striking thing for us, however, was what we saw in their daughters. They are maturing believers who are already engaging in cross-cultural missions. Their parents have done the hard work of discovering how to go from godless to godly patterns for living. And they took pains to pass what they were learning on to their daughters. These girls grew up beneficiaries of the healing their parents struggled to gain. They are beginning just about where their parents will leave off.

Millions of families around the world show similar conditions. The parents are believers in Christ, and so are the children—but often that's about as far as it goes. The difference with Dalby and Jane is that they have given their daughters a vision for being fruitful as insiders. They grew up watching Mom and Dad draw the people around them into the kingdom of God, and they listened to them talk about why they were giving themselves to this. When we see physical and spiritual generations converge in this manner, we know the kingdom of God is at hand and gathering momentum in its advance.

Where Did I Go Wrong?

WE HAVE SEEN how the Scriptures support the idea that God's workings with mankind follow the lines of physical and spiritual generations. So where did I go wrong in those early days?

My primary mistake was to pursue the idea of generations before I had an adequate biblical foundation to support it. Consequently, I set out to do ministry *my way*. I was individualistic. And my timing was *way* off.

Individualism

Somewhere I had gotten the idea that these generations needed to be *mine! I* needed to win and disciple people to validate *my own* fruitfulness. I needed to be able to point to certain people and claim them as *my* spiritual generations. I was ignoring a primary truth concerning the body of Christ. The body metaphor itself says it all. No single part can accomplish anything by itself. Growth occurs as "each part does its work."[29] Such individualism is barren because it seeks its own glory.

I grew up believing individualism was a virtue! Wasn't it our rugged individualism that made America great? I carried this idea over into my spiritual life. For years I read the Bible in the first person singular. Whenever it said "you," I took it to mean "me." Then I learned Portuguese. In Portuguese, there is both a plural and a singular form for the pronoun "you." I discovered that most of my favorite passages—that I had understood to be talking about *me*—were in the plural, talking about *us*, together!

As I began to align my life with this truth and as I learned to put my gifts and abilities to work along with those of a few other sisters and brothers, I began to experience true fruitfulness.

Time Frame

Another error I made was in the area of timing. I had false expectations for how long it should take for one spiritual generation to beget another. A year seemed like a reasonable span of time. Working in the American evangelical culture as I did for several years, I could sustain such an illusion! That was because almost everyone I ministered to already had some biblical heritage, sort of like the people at Pentecost!

Then we found ourselves in Brazil ministering to people who had never held a Bible in their hands. We found that the first year with those people would be invested in sowing the idea that Jesus was God. It would take another year for people to decide to follow him. Then they needed to deal with the basic issues of godliness in their personal lives: their marriages, careers, and all the rest that goes with living life. All this, of course, would take more years. True, many of their friends who were watching would also be drawn to Christ at the same time. But that's not multiplication. That's just a bit of spontaneous combustion! A generational ministry runs much deeper than that. Its goal is new, responsible, spiritual parenthood.

To lay foundations for new generations takes time. Too much time, you say? It may seem so at first, but in the end a life purposefully lived with a vision for generations can outstrip everything else. Its influence continues long after our life comes to an end! Because such a ministry follows the lines of social and family relationships, the impact, over time, tends to expand into new circles rather than run out.

GENERATIONS AND THE INSIDER

THE CLOSER YOU follow Christ, the greater will be your longing to see the people around you, especially your own family members, come into possession of the same gift you received from God. But often this natural desire is filled with frustration. Sometimes it seems so hopeless. We're at a loss as to how to proceed. A vision for generations provides a way forward. It means:

- seeing the world from where we are—an insider to a limited but boundary-less circle. It is understanding that there is no limit to where the fruit of our life could lead over the generations.

- intentionally discipling our children; giving priority to passing on to them the spiritual legacy we have received, with the vision that they, too, will embrace their calling to do the same. This is the greatest gift a parent can give a child. It is the gift of life and hope.
- purposefully investing deeply in a few individuals, with the expectation that God will, in time, multiply that investment.

CHAPTER 4

THE INSIDER

* * *

SO, JACK, WHAT *IS* IT ALL ABOUT?

We've seen that God has engaged us in the work he's doing. He's creating a *people* and he is working through us to do it. As these people are gathered to him, they are being given citizenship in God's kingdom. They're still here among us, but they already belong to another place. You can tell by the way they live that they're not from around here.

God has been putting this eternal extended family, this household, together for centuries. Much of the time he has followed bloodlines—from parents to children to grandchildren, then on out to neighbors and neighboring nations. Physical and spiritual generations converge to declare the rule of Christ to the world. Ultimately, this family will include people from every nation on earth.

Once we understand these things, we have the needed framework for understanding the *insider* and the critical role this person plays in the work God is doing. In this chapter we will define what we mean by *insider* and work through the biblical basis for the concept.

Christ's Body in the World

"THE BODY OF Christ!" This frequently used metaphor for the church takes us a long way toward understanding the place of the insider in the work God is doing: "Now you are the body of Christ, and each one of you is a part of it."[1] Spiritual birth into the family of God is marked by the Holy Spirit's entry into our life. He comes bearing gifts. Nobody is passed over. Each person is gifted by God's design. These gifts are not really for the person who receives them. They are for the body, for "to each one the manifestation of the Spirit is given for the common good."[2] We are to use these gifts along with our natural talents, abilities, and resources to serve the family of God and the people who surround them. The result is that the body "grows and builds itself up in love, as each part does its work."[3] Every believer has a part in the ministry. Contemporary theology refers to this as "the priesthood of the believer."

Many Christians tend to assume this gifting is an in-house service for use within the body. It is broader than that, because the affairs of God's people are broader than that. We are the *body* of Christ. We are his way of getting around in this world today! We are to use what we have both within God's family and in our society, among the people that surround us. Jesus made this clear in the things he taught and in the way he lived.

The Things Jesus Taught

Jesus assumed our insidership. As you read the Gospels, observe how much he had to say about how we ought to relate to the unbelievers around us. Jesus explained his own mission with the simple phrase, "The Son of Man came to seek and to save what was lost."[4] From the start he repeatedly made it clear that his people were to share in this same mission. What do you suppose he was telling us with his metaphors, "You are the salt of the earth," and "You are the light of the world"?[5] Jesus used these word pictures to communicate distinctiveness and visibility. He is saying, "Let me tell you why you are here. You're here to be salt-seasoning that brings out the God-flavors of this earth. If you lose your saltiness how will people taste godliness? . . . You're here to be light, bringing out the God-colors in the world. God is not a secret to be kept. We're going public with this, as public as a city on a hill."[6] "Let your light shine before men, that they may see your good deeds and praise your Father in heaven."[7] We are in the world to reveal Christ to the world. He is saying, Let it show!

Then he goes on to say there are other things we keep hidden. He says, "Be careful not to do your 'acts of righteousness' before men, to be seen by them."[8] He's talking about giving, praying, and fasting. In each case he says the same thing: Do it, but don't let anyone catch you at it! Why on earth not? The reason being, there were people in that crowd listening to him who spent their lives going from one religious activity to another. They imagined they were earning "travel points" to heaven. They also made sure everybody around them knew how devout they were. The rest of the society was both intimidated and disgusted by their lives. Jesus was confronting these people because they gave God a bad reputation.

We will always have an audience. People watch what Christians do and don't do, and on that basis decide whether or not they are interested in what we have. What unbeliever wants to spend his life praying, skipping meals, and giving his money away? It's not our religious activities we want people to see; it's the grace and mercy that comes from God's love that needs to show.

The Gospels are filled with instructions of this sort. Jesus repeatedly instructs us to live out what we have before the people we rub shoulders with every day, among whom we live as an *insider*. He tells us to love our enemies,[9] to direct our hospitality toward those who need him,[10] and to love our neighbors as ourselves.[11]

We have all heard of the popular notion that when Jesus calls a person, he is to drop whatever he is doing to go follow him. If you're serious about following Christ, the notion goes, you'll prepare to be a pastor or a missionary. Jesus did ask twelve people to drop what they were doing. "Come follow me," he said to them, "and I will make you fishers of men."[12] They left their work and followed him.

But what about the rest of his disciples? For them, his instructions were more the opposite. After he cured the man possessed by multiple demons, he told him, "Go home to your family and tell them how much the Lord has done for you."[13] We somehow find the idea of dropping everything to follow Jesus more romantic than that of our taking him back home with us. But as a rule, we are called to follow him back into our own communities. This book has to do with what that means.

One of Jesus' parables gives an especially succinct picture of the place of God's people in this world. It's the parable of the weeds.[14] The story is about a farmer who sowed good seed in his field. Then at night an enemy sowed weed seeds in the same field. The farmhands asked, What should we do now? Do we try to separate the two, or what? The instruction was to let them grow together. Everything will be sorted out at the end of the age. Jesus was making the point that, for now, the place for the children of the kingdom (the good seed) is in the world, right alongside the sons of the evil one. We are to live kingdomly in the midst of this lost world.

The Way He Lived

Jesus illustrated these ideas we've just seen by the way he lived his life. His behavior scandalized many: "The Pharisees and the teachers of the law muttered, 'This man welcomes sinners and eats with them.'"[15] The things Jesus taught about how we are to live in this world were illustrated by the way he lived. He had a reputation for being good friends with some very lost people.

When Jesus chose Levi as one of the Twelve, it must have raised a lot of eyebrows. Levi was a "publican" or tax collector, a Jew who collected revenue for the Romans. Publicans had the reputation for being corrupt—better to keep your distance from such people. If you really wanted to say something derogatory about another, you would call him a publican.[16]

Sometime after Jesus had called him, Levi went back home and threw a party for all his old friends. His featured guests were Jesus and the other disciples. This was a major event, a banquet and a reception. I assume he did this out of concern for his old friends, whom he wanted to meet Jesus too!

They were a rough crowd. Mark's account of the event reads, "When the teachers of the law who were Pharisees saw him eating with the 'sinners' and tax collectors, they asked his disciples: 'Why does he eat with tax collectors and "sinners"?'"[17] Jesus' behavior bothered them. After all, a person is known by the company he or she keeps. And, look at him comfortably sitting there, eating! He must have something in common with them! That would be the only logical conclusion. In that culture, eating with others was an expression of *koinonia*. We translate this "fellowship" or "to hold in common." To eat with another was an act of identification with the other person.

Jesus, the perfect one, knew how to put the worst of us at ease in his company.

THE INSIDER IN THE EPISTLES

THE SAME IDEA runs through the Epistles. They, too, are filled with instructions on how to live among the people who make up our everyday life. For example, in his letter to Christians in Philippi, Paul uses the same metaphor Jesus did: "Do everything without complaining or arguing, so that you may become blameless and pure, children of God without fault in a crooked and depraved generation, in which you shine like stars in the universe as you hold out the word of life."

Paul understood that he and his team could plant the gospel in a city but they could never hope to carry it into the heart of that society. They came in as *outsiders* to the city. They could reach a few. But those they did reach would, in turn, need to carry it back into their networks of relationships. So, his instruction to live blamelessly and to "hold out the word of life" was of utmost importance. The success or failure of the Apostle's efforts in Philippi rode on the believers responding to this challenge. Thus, Paul continues, do this "in order that I may boast on the day of Christ that I did not run or labor for nothing."[18]

The first generation of believers in Corinth was an especially needy bunch. In his first letter, Paul addresses some of their problems. They were quarreling with each other; there was jealousy, arrogance, immorality, lawsuits, and who knows what else! Undoubtedly, the fact that they lived surrounded by pagan temples, idol worship, and immorality of many kinds explains a lot of why they had the problems they did. The gospel is not a magic wand that makes our sins and vices disappear from one day to the next. It delivers us, a step at a time, as we walk with the Holy Spirit.

Apparently, there were some in Corinth who were trying to resolve their problems by withdrawing from them, by just changing their scenery. A believing husband—whose unbelieving wife would continue to do her daily rituals to her gods—would finally get sick of it and contemplate leaving her. Or, the believing wife would struggle over the idea of her husband continuing with the temple prostitutes, and she would want to leave him. To this, Paul wrote, "If any brother has a wife who is not a believer and she is willing to live with him, he must not divorce her. And if a woman has a husband who is not a believer and he is willing to live with her, she must not divorce him." Why not? Well, Paul says, there are children involved, and "How do you know, wife, whether you will save your husband? Or, how do you know, husband, whether you will save your wife?" Then he makes the very intriguing comment, "Each one should retain the place in life that the Lord assigned to him and to which God has called him."

Paul is saying we are to view our spouse and family as a part of our calling.

He continues, now talking about our social identities: "Was a man already circumcised [a Jew] when he was called? . . . Was a man uncircumcised [a gentile] when he was called?" Stay the way you are! Here Paul makes this same statement a second time: "Each one should remain in the situation which he was in when God called him." In other words, don't alter your social identity unnecessarily when you put your faith in Christ. God has something for you right where you are.

Then Paul moves to the subject of work. "Were you a slave when you were called? Don't let it trouble you—although if you can gain your freedom, do so." But you have already been bought with a price. You're free!

Here, a third time, Paul makes the same statement: "Each man, as responsible to God, should remain in the situation God called him to."[19] The work environment is but one more arena in which God can be glorified.

Are you looking for your calling, wondering what God wants you to do? Paul is saying, open your eyes and look! You're surrounded! You've spent thirty years relating to your family, your community, and your work situation. Some of your relationships are good, some are bad, but they all have potential for new meaning now that you're a citizen of the kingdom of God. Live out that citizenship—"hold out the word of life"[20] within this unique world of yours! That's what it means to be an *insider!*

All too frequently, however, the opposite becomes the rule. The new believer is led to understand that now he or she has become a part of the believing community and therefore needs to leave the old life. Does the Bible not say, "Come out from them and be separate. . . . Touch no unclean thing"?[21] Are we not warned that "bad company corrupts good character"?[22] On the basis of these and other Scriptures, it is often taught that believers should not have friendships with unbelievers. So there is a tension here. On one side we are told to stay where we are when we believe in Christ. On the other we are told to get away from people who will be bad influences. The Scriptures seem to build a case for both sides. How do we resolve this?[23]

FINDING THE BALANCE

MORE OFTEN THAN not, a wrong teaching is a half-truth. We take a biblical idea and carry it to its *illogical* conclusion, and we are misled. The error can be in the overemphasis of one side against the other. This issue is of that nature. The Scriptures that talk about believers needing to separate from the world were penned by the same person who instructed people to stay where they were. Is the apostle Paul contradicting himself, or do the two ideas fit together?

Obviously, there is truth on both sides, just as there is room for extremes on both sides. The Apostle is not teaching that a spouse must stay in an abusive relationship no matter how bad it gets. He is not saying that if your old crowd shoots up on drugs whenever they meet, you should keep hanging out with them, or that if you're working for the Mafia when you come to believe in Christ, that's where you belong! He is communicating a principle, not setting a law. He is writing to people who are living dull, gray lives made up of bad marriages, difficult working conditions, and low social esteem. He is saying, Don't worry about changing your circumstances. Through you, God has just invaded new territory! Through you the life of the invisible Christ can now be visible to the people around you. They don't have to go anywhere or join anything to see Christ, because you're there!

So how do we find this balance? We need to be careful not to draw the line between "separating" and "remaining" for other people. We do need to draw lines for ourselves, but that is as far as it can go. When I extend my personal boundaries to another I am a legalist. That is because separation, in the end, is a matter of the heart rather than of observing rules or maintaining certain physical distances.

Jesus, in praying for his disciples, said, "Sanctify them by the truth; your word is truth. As you sent me into the world, I have sent them into the world. For them I sanctify myself, that they too may be truly sanctified."[24] To sanctify (*hagiazo*) is to "set apart for sacred use." One does not lose, or gain one's sanctification by changing geography. It is a matter of who, or what, has one's heart. Every person needs to work out his or her own position, in his or her own heart, before God.[25]

WATCH YOUR FIELD POSITION!

OVER THE YEARS much has been written on the importance of believers keeping a safe distance from the world. Very, very little, however, has been said about the other side of the issue—the importance of believers remaining where they are, as insiders to their communities. In fact, this possibility is usually not even considered. Frequently, when people become Christians they are encouraged, directly or indirectly, to make immediate, radical changes in their worlds of relationships. Thus when they put their faith in Christ, that's the last their old friends ever see of them. As they withdraw they forfeit one of their best assets, their excellent field position. They trade it for an impossible one! Thus the person God intends to be an *insider* becomes an *outsider.* This same fault is committed repeatedly, all over the world.

Prior to his becoming a Christian, Mike was involved in politics and rugby. He enjoyed a unique world of relationships that included everyone from blue-collar, hard-drinking athletes to the prime minister of New Zealand. Yet within two years of becoming a Christian, he had become so busy in Christian activities he was unavailable to his old friends. They drifted off. No one even suggested that he might be doing something wrong, that he might consider staying in there and continue to give attention to his unbelieving friends.

Looking back on it now, Mike observes, "My experience is not unusual. The vital part insiders play in God's work is still undervalued and marginalized. Insiders are not missionary biography material. They don't even make the church bulletin! Yet they are key to what God is about in this world today."

We must do better than that! Insiders are essential to our accomplishing the ministry of the church, but too often we never give them a thought! This same neglect has extended into our global missionary efforts—and that has cost us dearly. Frequently, we have passed on to the churches that our missionaries have planted around the world this *genetic defect* that causes barrenness in their spiritual offspring. This is the subject of our next chapter.

CHAPTER 5

THE INSIDER'S ROLE
IN MISSIONS

* * *

Over the past two hundred years, the Western church has demonstrated its commitment to Christ's commission to take his good news to the nations of the world. Thousands of people have invested their lives by going as missionaries to foreign cultures, while many more have generously supplied the funds to make this possible. If we could add up this investment over these centuries, we would be staggered by the totals.

Only eternity will reveal the returns on this investment. I am sure we will also be amazed at all God has done over these years through it. But one thing is sure: the returns could be far greater. Because the role of the insider has not been a part of the *genetic code* of our sending churches, we would hardly expect to find it in our missionary churches either, as our missionary efforts are reflections of ourselves, for better or for worse. In them we see our own strengths and weaknesses. The omission of the insider is costing our missionaries growth of the gospel in many places.

In this chapter we will get a glimpse of what this omission is costing our missionaries. And whether we realize it or not, we are paying a similar price here at home.

We took the elevator to the sixth floor in a ten-story apartment building that was indistinguishable from several other buildings surrounding it. I was in the Spanish city of Barcelona, visiting a handful of young professionals who had come to faith in Christ as students and had then migrated into the city in pursuit of employment. One of them had developed a friendship with an American missionary family. He had soon realized they were struggling. The family had been in the city for five years seeking to plant a church, but had seen almost no fruit. Understandably, they were discouraged, and my friend hoped our visit would be helpful.

As we had tea together in their living room they related their story. When they had become functional in the Spanish language the husband began to go from door to door in the neighborhood offering literature, seeking to share the gospel, and inviting people to attend their church service. But after several years of knocking on countless doors they had virtually nothing to show for their efforts.

On Sundays they had a church service in their apartment. They had made friends with another family in the building and their children played together. The wife and children came over on Sunday mornings. The husband didn't. He had told them he wasn't interested in religion. Another single girl living in the next building also attended occasionally. She's a Protestant.

As we talked I noticed a stack of maple-wood folding chairs alongside the piano and a pile of paperback songbooks on the top of it. On Sunday mornings they would sing some songs, pray, and then they would have a meditation on a passage of Scripture. Because their goal was to plant a church, they reasoned, they needed a worship service to invite people to.

Missionary work in Spain has to be among the most difficult things one could possibly choose to do with one's life. It is as if the almost four hundred years of inquisition in Spanish history have done a spiritual lobotomy on the people.[1] God is not in their thoughts! Perhaps they find him just too terrifying to contemplate. Add to this picture the post-modernity that has swept into Europe and its chilling effects upon the church, and you get the idea. It is never easy in Spain, but these missionaries had wandered into an approach that was as much a barrier, in itself, as was the spiritual climate!

STACKING MARBLES

MOST CHRISTIANS ARE accustomed to congregating. They know what to expect when they attend a church service. But we forget how hard that can be for the uninitiated. Few of us are comfortable in a room full of people of diverse backgrounds whom we have never met before. In new situations where we have little natural affinity with the others, we worry: *What am I going to talk about? Will someone ask me embarrassing questions?* And we are sure everyone there will know more about what's going on than we do. It's just easier to stay away.

Spain is a relational society. Life travels along the lines of family, friendships, and relational networks. This missionary family was attempting to make new connections with new people every day. They were asking people they didn't know to traverse a forbidding social distance to participate in something of dubious interest to them. That's like trying to stack marbles, or like trying to get a few atoms that naturally repel each other to come together to form a critical mass.

If church-planting missionaries operate from a congregational blueprint, their notion of "church" can be among their biggest obstacles. They will be measuring their progress according to how many people they are succeeding in gathering into one place. They will tend to be thinking in terms of activities and forms rather than about people's relational networks.

Every individual becomes "one more!" Under those conditions, even if they are successful in gathering a congregation, even a large congregation, they are probably sabotaging the future generations of that body of believers! They are expecting people to disconnect from their relationships to join their church. This usually implies a change in identity for those people, which their family and friends interpret as one more sign of rejection. The prospects of a second generation drop to about zero!

SO WHAT DOES ONE DO?

THE INSIDER IS a key player in God's pursuit of the nations. If a church planter wants to end up with insiders who carry the gospel into their families and circles of friends, he needs to begin there, with that idea in mind. This is illustrated in the ministries of both Jesus and the Apostles.

The "man of peace" is one example, among many, from Jesus' ministry.

THE MAN OF PEACE

ON ONE OCCASION Jesus selected seventy-two people and sent them on ahead of him, two by two, into the villages he was planning to visit. They were to get people ready for his arrival. He gave them very specific instructions on what to say, what to do and not do, and what to take with them on their trips. Don't take money, he told them. And don't pack a bag. When you arrive in a town look for a "man of peace." Stay with him and his household for as long as you're in town. Accept their hospitality. Eat their food and sleep in their beds. Don't move around. Spend your days telling people what to expect when I get there. For credentials, I'm giving you the authority to perform miracles.[2]

Subsequently, when Jesus arrived in a town, people did show up! When he went into Capernaum, "so many gathered that there was no room left, not even outside the door."[3] And in another place it says, "So many people were coming and going that they [Jesus and the disciples] did not even have a chance to eat."[4] Jesus was sowing broadly in those days. He wasn't reaping very much. Apparently, people weren't ready for that. He never did reap large numbers.[5]

Where did this "man of peace" fit into Jesus plans? The text doesn't tell us anything more. We can imagine the two visitors arriving in a town, asking around for a certain kind of person. As they would pass people on the street they would say, We're looking for someone. No, we've never met him ourselves. No, we don't know his name, but he . . . People would listen, look at each other and say, Yeah, we know a guy like that. Lives down the street and to the left after you pass the big tree beyond the well.

This "man of peace" already had the attention of the townspeople for the kind of person he was. I think Jesus was laying the groundwork for the future by sending that man, and his household, those two unforgettable guests!

Cornelius, a Roman centurion, was a "man of peace." "He and all his family were devout and God-fearing; he gave generously to those in need and prayed to God regularly. . . . [He was] respected by all the Jewish people."[6] God sent Peter to bring the gospel to him and his household. When Peter entered Cornelius's house he found that "Cornelius was expecting them and had called together his relatives and close friends."[7] The house was full of people already marked by Cornelius's godly character. They were prepared—predisposed to believe the gospel when they heard it. Christ would build his church around people like that.

OUTSIDERS AND INSIDERS

IN GIVING US the Scriptures, the Holy Spirit made sure we got a clear picture of the life and ministry of the apostle Paul. His story occupies seventeen chapters of the book of Acts. And he wrote thirteen of the twenty-one letters preserved in our New Testament. I don't believe God intends that we try to reconstruct Paul's activities today or copy the forms he used, but we had better learn all we can from what he did and taught!

Paul's whole strategy hung on the insider. He accomplished his work through an apostolic team, a handful of gifted men, available to co-labor with him as he took the gospel to people "where Christ was not known."[8] The little team of apostles, "sent ones," would come into a town as *outsiders*. They had never before met the people they would be seeking to reach. Given this circumstance, their goals were limited. Their first objective was to lay foundations. Paul wrote, "By the grace God has given me, I laid a foundation as an expert builder."[9] For Paul, a foundation in this case meant a few people related to Christ and to one another—and who shared a common calling.

A foundation is an incomplete work, really quite useless in itself. Something needs to be built upon it before its value can be realized. And so it was with this apostolic ministry. Paul clearly understood that his success in a place was dependent upon what the people who made up the foundation did once his part was finished. In a letter to the believers in Corinth he wrote, "We . . . confine our boasting to the field God has assigned to us, a field that reaches even to you. . . . We did get as far as you with the gospel of Christ. . . . Our hope is that, as your faith contin- ues to grow, our area of activity among you will greatly expand, so that we can preach the gospel in the regions beyond you."[10]

So he watched the believers in Corinth to see what would happen next. We did get as far as you, he said. Now we're counting on you to take it from there. In his mind, an effort wasn't a success until he could see the gospel growing in lives (as evidenced by faith, hope, and love) and then outward among the people around them.[11] Only then did he feel free to concentrate on getting to other regions.

Paul understood that if there was going to be an impact by the gospel in a place, it would have to be through the people of that place more than through the apostolic team. The team could get things started but only insiders could make the good news flow through their relational networks. And they would be there long term to see spiritual generations birthed and grown to maturity.

It is no surprise, then, that Paul's letters are filled with instructions on how to make the most of one's insidership. For example, to the believers in Ephesus he wrote,

> You were once darkness, but now you are light in the Lord.
> Live as children of light (. . . in all goodness, righteousness and
> truth) . . . for it is light that makes everything visible. This is
> why it is said:
>> "Wake up, O sleeper,
>> rise from the dead,
>> and Christ will shine on you."[12]

With this metaphor, Paul is comparing the presence of a truly Christlike, believing community with someone turning floodlights on in the middle of the night inside a dormitory filled with sleeping people. The light will awaken the sleeper, who will certainly ask what's going on. So, he continues, as that happens, "Be very careful, then, how you live . . . making the most of every opportunity."[13]

TURNING ON THE LIGHTS

I WAS ON my way to Bangkok and had to lay over in Singapore. The next morning found me sitting at a sidewalk table drinking coffee. The streets were teeming with people headed for work. As I watched them stream past, I began to pray. I would pick one out in the crowd and ask God to bring something into that life that would reveal Christ to him or her. I was going from one to another. Then I found myself wondering what might that "something" be? Where, how, I wondered, could this mass of people have access to the news about Christ in such a way that they could understand and believe? I prayed, Lord, if there are any quicker, better ways than the ones I have learned, I want to know about them.

I thought about our most predictable response to that question: Do a citywide crusade! True, I thought, that would reach a few. It would be a selected few. What about the rest? We could put the media to work, I thought. Use radio and television. I have seen these serve as wonderful resources, especially in hard places. They sow where people can't go. But looking at those people streaming past I had to admit that most would never stop to pay attention to any of these efforts—because it is dark where they are. The floodlights have to come on first. That means another person, whom they know and trust and in whom they see something of Christ, needs to arrest their attention. The gospel needs to be seen *and* heard to be understood by most people.

And in Barcelona . . .

THE MISSIONARY FAMILY in Barcelona illustrates the things we are talking about in this chapter. They didn't recognize that possibly their best opportunity was already right in front of them. Their children were friends with those of another family. The parents had become acquainted. They had something in common. At that point, rather than trying to convene an activity the husband had no interest in, they should have done the opposite. They should have made the effort to get to know him, to build some bridges between the families.

As the friendship developed, that husband, who didn't like religion, could have mentored them into a way forward that might fit even him. One's mentor in such a circumstance doesn't need to be a believer. In fact, I've found it is sometimes better when they aren't. They can tell you how your life looks from the street!

All it would have taken to get this valuable input would have been to ask a few good questions and be good listeners. In time, if the missionary couple passed the test, they would naturally be introduced to others in that family's network. By nurturing a few more friendships of this same sort, they could be on their way—granted, slowly! And they would probably never use those folding chairs and songbooks!

People who are predisposed to believe, like Cornelius, are rare to nonexistent in countries such as Spain. God needs to lead us to those few, but we need to know what to look for.

Rethinking Our Approach

OVER THE PAST few decades much research has been devoted to locating and identifying the tribes and "people groups" of the world. As a result, today we know where to find people we had never even heard of until recently. But we're still short on knowing what to do to move the gospel into those cultures once we get there. Even most books written for missionaries on church planting are silent on the place of insiders in seeing this happen.

Insiders are at the heart of God's pursuit of the nations. They are essential to what he wants to do. Yet, in many churches and missions efforts they face resistance and disapproval rather than support. They are made to feel they are somehow disloyal because of the time and space they give their unbelieving friends. What they need instead is affirmation, equipping, and resourcing—and lots of it.

CHAPTER 6

INSIDERS AND THEIR CHURCHES

* * *

Being an insider is as much a part of the mission of the church as its foreign missions endeavors. The apostle Paul depended on insiders to pick up where his team left off in a city. The insiders had the connections, the relationships, the trust. They could take the gospel into the heart of their society. Does it not follow that the same should hold true for the churches in our cities today? For some reason we don't often think in those terms. In fact, I meet a lot of people who are reaching out to their unbelieving friends as insiders and, for one reason or another, feel they are at cross-purposes with their church. They feel tension!

Ron and Liz grew up with many of the ideas we are expressing in this book. Liz's parents put their faith in Christ in midlife when a friend invited her mother to read the Bible with her. From then on her parents lived with their door open to their unbelieving friends. Ron and Liz follow a similar lifestyle.

A few years ago Ron and Liz realized that the small town they were living in was keeping them marginalized in their efforts as insiders. Life was comfortable. They knew everyone around them. Most were Christians. So they decided to move! They wanted to be in a place where their light would be more needed.

They moved to another city, into a new neighborhood, and began to connect with their new neighbors. And their children, who are now close to adulthood, joined them in this calling. The inevitable has happened. The family now finds itself at the hub of a growing, far-reaching network of other insiders, new believers, and pre-believers. And they are trying to figure out what to do next.

The easy, predictable, answer would be to start a church. This, in fact, is how many of the churches we have today got started. But Ron and Liz don't want to do that. They are now positioned to carry the gospel much further into their world of relationships. Their networks are too loose and too far-reaching to constitute a congregation. If they did that they would just lose too much. What they really need is to be resourced. They need affirmation and encouragement. They need people who understand and are experienced in what they're doing to coach them in what to do next and how to do it. They need prayer.

Meanwhile, their church is wondering what has happened to Ron and Liz. Previously they could always be counted upon to teach a class, serve on a board, or be on a committee. Now all they seem to do is attend. In fact, there are times when they don't even do that! By all appearances, they have lost their loyalty. It's hard not to criticize them!

TENSION!

THIS LOOKS LIKE a simple breakdown in communication. There are frustrations on both sides. The insider feels it—and so do the leaders of the church. One would think this breakdown could be resolved by everyone sitting down together and reaching a mutual understanding. Sometimes that is all it takes, but at other times it is not that simple.

Being an insider requires a change in venue. It requires connecting with people *where* they are, on their turf, and at times *when* they are available. Some unbelievers will respond to the idea of participating in the activities of the church, but increasingly large segments of our society will not. This can be very difficult for many of us to understand and accept. What we have works for us in our church, we reason, and we can't imagine why it wouldn't work for others as well!

Part of our difficulty is in our popular definition of church. It has become a place where people meet for certain activities.[1] Our sense of identity has shifted from being a people who are sent into the world to being a place where people congregate to worship. Given this definition, the activities of the insider will become very difficult to understand. And insiders, in turn, lose their sense of belonging, as their calling will not fit within the walls.

We are confronted here with a conflict of priorities. For one, the primary concern is the care of the believing community. For the other, the main issue is the unbelieving world that surrounds them. Which is *the* priority? Is it ministry to the saints, or is it mission to the lost? That's like asking which wing of a bird is most important, the right or the left! Both are needed if the bird is going to fly. Our problem is that we seem to have great difficulty using both of them at the same time. I think there is an historical explanation for why this is so.

NOT PART OF OUR HISTORY

THE CHURCH WENT from its obscure beginnings as a movement within the Jewish community in Palestine to becoming the official religion of the Roman Empire within a space of three hundred years. It's an amazing story! Then, Constantine's edict of toleration, reportedly issued in Milan in A.D. 313, marked a turning point for the church. Within a few decades it went from being a persecuted sect to an instrument of the state; from being anti-society to being the guardian of the society.[2]

Imagine the challenges the church faced at that juncture! The leaders of the church were suddenly called upon to regularize virtually every aspect of society, as Constantine was intent on making the church a buttress of his state. To accomplish this, to create a total Christian society, required making church membership compulsory. People could no longer choose whether or not they wanted to belong. They were baptized into the church at birth. With this the idea of an unbelieving society that needed to be evangelized was lost. There were only good church members and bad church members. Bad members faced the wrath of the state. The church and the state served each other toward the common goal of maintaining the imperial state. This relationship remained unchallenged over the next millennium, until the Reformation.

There were four primary strands within the Protestant Reformation: the Lutheran, the Reformed, the Anglican, and the Anabaptist. There was also a corresponding counter-reformation within the Catholic Church. Only two of these, the Anabaptists and the Catholic counter-reformations, even came close to addressing the issue of the mission of the church. Mission was not among the concerns of the reformers of the sixteenth century.[3]

What occupied Martin Luther was the corruption he saw within the church. He challenged the sale of indulgences and the idea of amassing good works through pilgrimages, fasting, confessions, and calling on saints. His experience of personal forgiveness, the discovery that salvation is through faith, opened up his understanding of God's grace and the forgiveness of sins. This truth became the substance of the Protestant experience.[4] This insight, in turn, led him into his anticlerical defense of the priesthood of every believer. He also repositioned the Scriptures as the sole authority for life and practice.

Apparently, Luther never questioned the idea of a hierarchical, universal church that functioned in concert with the state. Neither did John Calvin. The churches that grew out of their work were adaptations of the church-state idea, essentially no different from medieval Christianity in their organization. Both continued to support the Augustinian concept of creating a city of God here on earth.[5] The same could be said of the Anglican Church. It was founded with King Henry VIII as its head, which again made the church and the state partners. Consequently, for these reformers, the church parish included the entire society. Everybody was in the church.

The Anabaptists, or the "free-church movement," were an exception. They stressed the idea that the church must be a voluntary fellowship of believers baptized to affirm their personal conversions. Church practice was to be patterned after the early church. People were saved or lost according to their personal choice. The Anabaptists endured fierce persecution from every quarter, from the Catholic Church and from the reformers—both Luther and Calvin. Their influence on the whole was therefore limited.

Thus, the predominant parties in the Reformation did not really break from the medieval understanding of a territorial church maintained through the church-state relationship. But the reformers did sow the seeds for an eventual rebirth of the mission of the church. Luther's rediscovery of the phrase "The righteous will live by faith"[6] served to clarify the fact that people are fallen and lost, and in need of personal salvation. His emphasis on the priesthood of all believers led to a new understanding that every believer has a calling and responsibility to serve God. Those seeds, sown at that time, took years to germinate and bloom. The reformers were occupied with other issues and battling for survival. They weren't ready to think about taking the gospel to the nations—or to the neighbor next door. It took another two hundred years for the churches of the Reformation to take action in foreign missions, and even longer to begin to really understand their local mission.

I believe we are still affected, as a church, by the twelve centuries of territorial Christendom, dating from Constantine's edict in 313 to the day in 1517 when Martin Luther nailed his ninety-five propositions on the door of All Saints' Church at Wittenberg. These are twelve centuries in our history during which the idea of sharing the good news of Christ with one's neighbor was not even in most of our theologies.

SIGNALS OF CHANGE

AS STATED, IT took two hundred years for the churches of the Reformation to begin to consciously act upon their calling to take the gospel to the nations. But the gospel had been set free! In those two centuries there were a series of great awakenings that resulted in hundreds of thousands of individual lives being transformed. Our civilization was marked by these awakenings. They helped to eventually awaken the church to its responsibility to engage in foreign missions. In 1792 the Baptist Missionary Society was organized in England. In 1793 they sent William Carey to Serampore, India, as their first missionary.[7]

The birthing of what is now the Methodist church is an example of such an awakening. John Wesley (1703–1791), his brother Charles (1707–1788), and their friend George Whitefield (1714–1770) formed a little club, the Holy Club, at Oxford University. It was nicknamed "Methodist" for its disciplined ways. This movement also grew through tireless itinerant preaching by both John and George. They gathered their converts into societies across England, Scotland, and Ireland. Jonathan Edwards's (1750–1815) influence is an example of another powerful awakening. Through his writing and preaching he fanned the flames of the gospel throughout England, Scotland, and also in New England.[8]

In the nineteenth century the church in America set out to take the gospel to its own society. Organizations like the American Bible Society, the

Home Missionary Society, and the American Sunday School Union were raised up for this purpose. The country has also seen a stream of countless itinerant evangelists, people who gave themselves as missionaries to winning nonChristians, especially in the cities of America. The names of many are well known—people such as Charles G. Finney and Dwight L. Moody.

Our church today continues to grow in its awareness of its calling to the lost. We see this being expressed in a variety of forms, some of which are very creative. In recent years there has been an emphasis on church planting, first in our foreign missionary efforts, and more recently, in our urban areas. The idea of the "seeker-friendly church" was inspired by the concept of church planting. This is an effort to attract unbelievers— who would normally not be interested—to attend a church designed especially for them. We are also experiencing a multiplication of support groups, home groups, and mini-churches that are intent on reaching into segments of our society that have special needs.

But There's More to Come

ALTHOUGH WE MIGHT be making progress in our understanding of our calling to the lost, we still suffer a hangover from our past history. We still aren't skilled at enabling believers to engage effectively with the unbelievers in their world. You will notice that most of these "signs of change" we just mentioned still depend upon "come to" and "listen to" approaches. This promotion of dependence affects the health of the church in two ways.

First, it leaves all but a few believers in a passive, observer role in the church's pursuit of its mission. And second, it underutilizes our most strategic resource to that mission, the believer who rubs shoulders daily with the very people God calls us to go to. These omissions take their toll on the general health of the church.

Over the past fifty years many churches have attempted to address this need by emphasizing discipleship. A disciple is someone who learns by following, listening to, and imitating a mentor. Discipleship is in our vocabulary and our programs today, but discipleship does not character-ize our churches. We, as a people, are not particularly intent on following Christ. Current statistics on churched versus unchurched behavior tell us that. Several factors are at work here, but one of these, for sure, is the subject of this chapter.

Simply put, the Reformation has yet to return the *ministry* to the laity. We got the Bible and the gospel back, but we are still waiting for the rest. It is difficult, as a follower of Christ, to stay focused and disci-plined year after year when the prospects of engaging in the front lines of our calling seem so remote. But when we can look around in the middle of our business day at coworkers we are praying for and know that the manner in which we do our work will be important to their further progress toward Christ, life takes on new meaning. This is what was at the heart of Jack's struggle. He was feeling that most of what went on in his everyday life was irrelevant to God's purposes. He needed help in understanding how to invest his life in what God is doing.

FREEDOM OF FORM

THERE IS REALLY nothing standing in the way for the church to move in the direction of empowering insiders other than the limitations of our own vision. We enjoy unusual freedom today to experiment and inno-vate. We take this freedom so much for granted that it is difficult for us to believe that throughout much of church history it did not exist. It was common for church leaders to forbid anything outside the orthodox pat-terns of doctrine and practice.

Today, we have the freedom to go to the Scriptures, examine our beliefs and practices in light of what we find and understand—and then go do it! This is both a great opportunity and a sobering responsibility. We can all tell stories of people who justify the most outlandish ideas with the Bible. We can make the Scriptures say anything we want them to if we aren't careful. The apostle Peter warns us that no Scripture "is a matter of one's own interpretation."[9] We need to search the Scriptures prayerfully, in dependence on the Holy Spirit and on one another. Then we must act accordingly. In this way, God will lead us into truth.

THE APOSTOLIC CALLING OF THE CHURCH

A GOOD STARTING point for understanding our mission is to review what Jesus had to say about it. In his prayer to his Father, just before he was arrested, Jesus said, "Now this is eternal life: that they may know you, the only true God, and Jesus Christ, whom you have sent. . . . They [the Twelve] believed that you sent me. . . . As you sent me into the world, I have sent them into the world. . . . I pray also for those who will believe in me through their message . . . that the world may believe that you have sent me."[10]

Jesus was the first apostle. He was sent by his Father. He, in turn, sent the Twelve. They went to people who would then take the gospel to the rest of the world. Whoever received it would understand that they, too, had been sent. With the gospel being what it is, the church as bearer of the gospel is bound to be apostolic. The definition of apostle is "a sending, a mission, signifies an apostleship."[11]

We as a people have been sent.

If that is true, we need to define and organize ourselves accordingly. In no way can we let our vision for the church be restricted to the particular body of believers with whom we fellowship. This is important for people like Ron and Liz. They can't predict where the people they reach will end up. If they are expected to bring those people into their particular local church, they will have to carry a double message: the good news about Christ and another about their church. That goes too far! It doesn't matter how great our church is, our gospel is no longer pure when that's the way we come across.

It is more difficult for us to live by this than we think. Darrell Guder and the coauthors of the book *Missional Church* make the point that in America the church is a voluntary association that "lives off the willingness of its members to remain in it."[12] This puts a local church in a position where it will be tempted to compete for its market share. Because our society lives on marketing, we are hardly aware when our church falls into the temptation. As costs for providing church as we know it soar, it becomes harder and harder to be openhanded with people. A possessive mentality works against insiders. The circle a church draws in defining itself must be large enough to accommodate the fruit of the insider's labor.

On one occasion, some of John the Baptist's disciples came to him to warn him that he was losing his followers to Jesus. He replied, "You yourselves can testify that I said, 'I am not the Christ.' . . . The bride belongs to the bridegroom." John is reminding us that the bride doesn't marry the best man, she takes on the name of the bridegroom. He continues, "He must become greater; I must become less."[13] In other words, our part is to make sure the wedding takes place. The people we reach don't become *ours*. They belong to Christ. When we are truly unconcerned about who gets the credit, it is amazing how worlds of people open up to the gospel.

When Giving Becomes Receiving

MIKE AND GAYELYNN have been following Christ for about a year. In this short time they have proven to be prolific insiders. Apparently, the contrast between what they were and what they are becoming in Christ is so striking that many of their friends are stopping to take notice. Mike and Gayelynn are learning to explain what is happening in their lives to these friends in ways that have them asking for more. Being overwhelmed with opportunity, Mike asked us—Mike Shamy and myself—for help.

Over the past three to four months, we have been meeting after-hours in the boardroom of Mike's office for a Bible study with some of his business associates. About a dozen men are involved. They showed up with enormous, brand-new NIV Bibles that have never been opened. We began by explaining that the big numbers on the page are called chapters and the little ones are called verses, that there are two testaments in the Bible, and so on.

We found it interesting that within a few weeks all of them were talking about the churches they have begun to visit or attend. They assume that church is to be a part of their new faith. But because every church has its own ethos, some feel good in one and others in another. Because people will gravitate toward others of their own kind, these men look around for a church of their own kinds of people. There are already a half-dozen churches in this city on the receiving end of this one couple's ministry as insiders.

It doesn't always happen this way. Unchurched people don't always naturally look for a church when they put their faith in Christ, especially in certain parts of the world. In some countries of postmodern Europe, for example, the church has become so marginal to the mainstream of the culture that when such people do come to believe in Christ they often don't find the existing churches to be viable places for them. It is better, in those situations, to help new believers become the community for one another.

Whichever solution we might turn to for providing community for new believers, the truth stands: There is one body, and every part needs to contribute to the whole. "The whole body . . . grows and builds itself up in love, as each part does its work."[14] We who make up the church of this generation need to tend to our God-given mission just as much as we need to tend to our ministering to one another. Insiders have a part to play in this mission that no one else can. The body needs them desperately. And they need the body in the same way! It is time to make room for them.

OVERCOMING THE OBSTACLES TO FRUITFULNESS

Part Two:

INTRODUCTION

* * *

We have looked at the work God is doing today and asked the questions: What does this tell us about God's purposes for us? Do we have a part in what he is doing? What does he have in mind for us?

We saw that God is creating. This time he is creating a *people*—an eternal people, gathered out of every generation and from every nation. He is creating them at the expense of a *cross*—to be his Son's inheritance. And, yes, we do have a part in this work.

From the outset, God has partnered with people. Perhaps he is doing it that way, engaging us in the project, because he knows we need the experience if we are to become fit members of his household. As we do his work, he shapes us into the kind of people he intends us to be.

His plan is long range. It was in place before creation commenced. It began to take obvious shape when God told Abraham, "All peoples on earth will be blessed through you."[1] The year was circa 2086 B.C. Abraham and his offspring, his sons and grandsons, were the seeds God used to produce this people. Then Jesus, the *seed* of Abraham, came into the world. Now we, through him, are Abraham's *children*. God works through people. We are today's seed for tomorrow's generations.

At the epicenter of this new creation we find a lone man, born into a common family, in a town in Galilee. He preached a kingdom nobody could see. Who, then, could imagine he was The King himself, and that he was proclaiming an eternal kingdom that extends over all that makes up this universe and puts an end to all evil.

We have been invited to participate in this matchless enterprise. We are already in position. We start where we are, with what we have: a unique set of relationships made up of family, social network, and workplace. We have the *inside* advantage in those relationships. Our next question is, Now what do we do? How do we fruitfully engage these people to the glory of God? We will be addressing this question through the rest of the book.

In this next section we will look at some of the obstacles we face as we pursue this calling. We will address four of these that are common to us all. They are:

1. Our struggles with fear: *What will people think?*
2. Questions of Christian conduct: *What if I'm asked to do things I think are wrong?*
3. Finding time in a time-starved life: *There is no space in my life for another thing!*
4. Our personal inadequacies: *I'm just not ready for this.*

CHAPTER 7

FROM FEAR TO FREEDOM

* * *

This idea, that we are surrounded by our field of service, is motivating. It is also unnerving! All kinds of thoughts rush into our mind as we contemplate what this calling might mean for us personally. We respond with thoughts like, *I'm not comfortable among unbelievers,* or *I don't know enough to do anything like that.* Others worry, *Where would I find the time?* Or we worry that we aren't qualified. *I don't have it together myself,* we think. *Who am I to be connecting with others when what I really need is for someone to be giving* me *a hand with what's going on in* my *life?*

There is one common thread that runs through all of these responses. It is *fear.* We have all sorts of fears, and fear paralyzes. Fear itself, therefore, is our first hurdle. We won't get much further until we face it.

THE PROBLEM OF FEAR

FEAR IS PROBABLY our most uncomfortable, unpleasant emotion. Fear and its derivatives—anxiety, stress, and worry—conspire to make our life uncomfortable. Yet we wouldn't survive without it. We wouldn't have made it into adulthood if we hadn't learned to respect things like hot stoves and electric wires. Fear still serves us. It got us out of the way of the oncoming traffic on our way to work today.

There are good fears and bad fears, and the link between the two is sometimes subtle, as healthy fears can easily become bad habits.

Over the years I have had the opportunity to observe missionaries working in dangerous places such as behind the Iron Curtain, in Muslim states, and in communist China. The very real prospect of being arrested by the secret police teaches these people to be cautious in the way they go about their work. Dangers and restrictions impose this caution.

Often, over time, caution and covertness become a way of life for these people. They are unaware that this is happening. They dream of being able to work openly and imagine what they would do if they could throw caution to the winds and just go for it. Then it happens! One day they wake up and find that the repressive regime is no more. Some seize the opportunity, but many do not. They have become so accustomed to their cages that they do not leave them—even when the door is open. Their fearful behavior is no longer based upon reason. It is habitual.

This is what fear does to us. It paralyzes and imprisons. Fears of the future, of failure, of success, of people, of flying, or of closed-in places conspire to keep us from pursuing our visions—or of enjoying this beautiful day!

Did you know that Christ died to deliver us from our fears? The author of the book of Hebrews wrote that Christ became a man so that "by his death he might destroy him who holds the power of death—that is, the devil—and free those who all their lives were held in slavery by their fear of death."[1]

Fear is basic to Satan's arsenal. He knows if he can get us to fear he won't have to worry about us anymore. He can go on to other things because we have been paralyzed. And he knows the fear of death is the easiest of all fears to evoke in us. Thus he gets us to do his will. The Bible is filled with stories of people who forfeited their calling because they were controlled by fear rather than faith.

For example, as Israel first neared the land God had promised to them, Moses sent twelve men to spy it out and bring back a report on what it was like. The twelve men were impressed with two things that they saw: the abundance of the land's produce and the formidability of its inhabitants. Ten of the twelve decided that by the looks of things, Israel was no match for the occasion. Two, however, Caleb and Joshua, saw the same things, but through the eyes of faith. Caleb's counsel was, "We should go up and take possession of the land, for we can certainly do it."[2]

The majority prevailed—and, consequently, several million people needlessly spent the next forty years making grand circles in the desert. At the end of those forty years, as they were again preparing to enter that land, Moses played back for them what had happened the first time around. He reminded them that they had complained, "Our brothers [the ten spies] have made us lose heart. They say, 'The people are stronger and taller than we are; the cities are large, with walls up to the sky.'" Then Moses reminded them of what he had told them in reply on that occasion. He had said, "Do not be terrified; do not be afraid of them. The LORD your God, who is going before you, will fight for you.'"[3]

Fear is contagious, and if you catch it, it will make your life a wasteland.

A MOST COMMON FEAR

JERRY AND DONNA were both raised in Christian homes. They have been married for ten years and have lived in their neighborhood for eight. They have two kids, four and six years old. Their marriage is okay, but not great. There are tensions. Often the atmosphere gets stormy. But they love each other and are learning to make life together work.

Two years ago they met Al and Eva, their neighbors who live across

the street, at a meeting of their neighborhood association. The two families have a lot in common. Both are originally from the Midwest. Their
jobs are similar and their children are of the same ages.

It didn't take Jerry and Donna long to realize that Al and Eva are in
trouble in their marriage. It doesn't look like it is going to last. The big thing
they learned, in their own marital struggles, is the power of forgiveness.
They know if Al and Eva could just learn this, their whole relationship could
turn around. But they have also learned that people don't have the ability to
freely forgive without first experiencing Christ's forgiveness. So they invited
them to attend church a couple of times. Their uninterested response killed
that idea and left Jerry and Donna feeling uncomfortable. They are withdrawing a bit from their friendship with Al and Eva. They don't want to get
in any deeper than they are. They explain, "We aren't comfortable talking
about religion. Today, it is so important to be tolerant of what others believe.
And, as you know, over the past years the image of evangelical Christianity
has taken a beating in the press. The subject has become taboo."

This fear of social rejection has been around a long time. Jesus
healed a man that had been blind from birth. Unable to work, the man
had become a familiar figure in town, always in the same spot, always
begging for a coin or two from those passing by. Then one day he could
see! People couldn't believe it. Maybe, they thought, it is someone else
dressed up to look like him. They called for his parents and asked, "Is
this the one you say was born blind? How is it that now he can see?"

"We know he is our son," the parents replied, "and we know he was
born blind." That was all they were willing to say. They concluded, "Ask
him. He is of age; he will speak for himself."[4]

How strange! One would expect the parents to be euphoric over what
had happened to their son. But instead they distanced themselves from
it all. Why? The text explains, "His parents said this because they were
afraid of the Jews, for already the Jews had decided that anyone who

acknowledged that Jesus was the Christ would be put out of the synagogue."[5] The parents feared they would lose their place in society! It was the same fear Jerry and Donna struggle with.

Jerry and Donna are indebted to the Holy Spirit for keeping their family in one piece. They are learning to respond with grace in everyday life together, yet they are paralyzed by the thought of passing this critical news on to another couple in need. Fear makes us irrational.

"NO FEAR"

SOMETIMES I WONDER what God could do through my life if I were totally fearless. But on second thought, I don't think that would be a good idea. I know a few fearless people—and I find myself wishing they *had* a little fear! They are so bold, so confrontational in their witness that I fear for my unbelieving friends when they come around. They find openings where none exist and, disregarding the listener's frantic "Let me out of here!" body language, they press on. When it's over I am left to comfort the wounded.

We need a bit of healthy fear in our social relationships in the same way that we need it as pedestrians crossing a busy intersection at rush hour. It provides us with enough caution for self-preservation. In our social relationships it reminds us to proceed in a way that values *rapport*.

Rapport says, I want to hear what you have to say. I am listening. A person who ignores the signals, who boldly proceeds regardless of whether there is rapport or not, often comes across as being verbally rude or inappropriate.

A BOLDNESS THAT ENHANCES RAPPORT

YET, BOLDNESS IS indispensable! We need to be bold. Jesus was bold, and the people who followed him picked it up. Luke writes, "When they saw the courage of Peter and John . . . they took note that these men had been with Jesus."[6]

More than once, the intrepid apostle Paul's primary prayer request was for boldness: "Pray also for me . . . so that I will fearlessly make known the mystery of the gospel."[7]

Boldness and rapport; we need them both. We need to maintain a healthy tension between the two, as either one without the other can cause us to fail. One can have all the rapport in the world with people, but it also takes words to bring someone to Christ. On the other extreme, we can boldly persist in talking to someone who has tuned us out. This person won't believe in Christ either.

As an insider, we have a restricted field of opportunity. We walk through that field daily and can count the people in it. If our notion of boldness is not seasoned with a quest for rapport, we risk polarizing those relationships. Then what do we do? Do we go find a new job? Do we move to a new neighborhood? What is appropriate boldness for an insider? Boldness is not always expressed in words.

I am a relatively shy person. I feel uncomfortable in certain situations—as in a room full of strangers at a party. I want to escape! My wife, Marge, is the opposite. She's at home with people she has never seen before. Conversations flow around her, while I stand there in dumb silence. She has a boldness that creates rapport because it comes out of a natural interest in people. She is quick to serve a total stranger in some little way, like helping the person get an arm into a coat. She has no agenda. Boldness in loving people is always appropriate. I have learned from her that when I'm bold in acting out of love for people, the right words follow much more easily.

Insiders need to learn to be bold in ways that enhance rapport. The apostle Paul, coaching the believers in the city of Colosse in their role as insiders, wrote, "Use your heads as you live and work among outsiders.

Don't miss a trick. Make the most of every opportunity. Be gracious in your speech. The goal is to bring out the best in others in a conversation, not put them down, not cut them out."[8]

FROM FEAR TO FAITH

FEAR IS INESCAPABLE. If we waited until we were fearless before we acted on God's call, we would be waiting until the day we die. The goal is not to be free from fear; rather it is to prevent fear from paralyzing our actions. Fear is not wrong. It is not sin. Look at what Paul has to say about it in his letter to the believers in Corinth.

> When I came to you, brothers, I did not come to you with elo-quence, or superior wisdom. . . . I came to you in weakness and fear, and with much trembling. My message and my preaching were not with wise and persuasive words . . . so that your faith might not rest on men's wisdom, but on God's power.[9]

Paul was not the fearless soul that we might imagine him to be. He just found a way not only to keep his fears from slowing him down, but to make them work in favor of the gospel! How do you suppose he did that? He gives us some clues in his letters. Let's look at three of them.

1. Be transparent about your fears.

This passage we just read is an example of how he used his fears to advantage. Paul let everybody know what was going on inside him. He laid his fears out before his brothers and sisters and asked them to join him in taking them to God in prayer. "Pray also for me," he wrote, "so that I will fearlessly make known the mystery of the gospel."[10]

Prayer is our first defense against fear. It didn't take long for the fledgling church to find themselves in trouble with the authorities in Jerusalem. The powers that be arrested Peter and John for disturbing the peace with their bold preaching and threatened them with further punishment if they continued.

Upon release, Peter and John rehearsed what had happened to the church. The people might have felt intimidated, but they went to prayer. They began their prayer with a review of whom it was they were talking to. "Sovereign Lord," they prayed, "you made the heaven and the earth and the sea, and everything in them." In the context of this review of who God is, they ended their prayer with these words: "Now, Lord, consider their threats and enable your servants to speak your word with great boldness."[11] When we examine our fears in the light of God's greatness they look much different.

So how do we deal with our fears? We worship God!

2. Ask God for the words you will need.

Our vague feelings of fear quickly become very specific when we know an opportunity to talk about Christ is about to happen. *What am I going to say?* we worry. If we only knew what to say it would be a lot easier.

The apostle Paul experienced this same fear, and he added it to his list of prayer requests. "Pray . . . that whenever I open my mouth, words may be given me . . . that I may declare it fearlessly, as I should."[12]

He prayed God would give him the words he would need, at the time he needed them. The believers under threat in Jerusalem prayed a similar request. They said, "Enable your servants to speak your word with great boldness."[13] We can trust God, in the midst of our fear, to give us the words!

The apostle Peter adds a word of wise counsel to this. He wrote, "Be prepared to give an answer to everyone who asks you."[14] Think about what you might say when an opportunity to tell your story about Christ comes your way. Work out your answers ahead of time.

I've found that the most fruitful time to do this is when I've just missed an opportunity. I do an instant replay. I reflect on what happened and think through what I could have said or done differently. The fact is, opportunities do reoccur. I want to be ready when they come around again.

3. Accept your fear as an opportunity.

Allow it to take you deeper in your dependence. Did you know your fears and weaknesses can work *for* you?

In one Scripture, the apostle Paul describes the important place his weaknesses have in his ministry. He had some debilitating physical problems that "tormented" him. Imagining how much more he could do if he were free of them, he prayed repeatedly that he would be healed. But God answered, "My power is made perfect in [your] weakness."[15] In other words, they made Paul so aware of his limitations he didn't even try to do things under his own power. He knew he had no alternative but to draw upon Christ's power. He concludes his explanation with the words, "When I am weak, then I am strong."[16]

Our fears can lead us into greater sensitivity to the Holy Spirit. Following God's leading inevitably puts us in frightening situations. He is bound to take us into things that are way over our head—into things only he can do. It has to be that way. How else would we learn about him? If we just stick to those things we could do anyway, where would the "God factor" be? If we refuse to follow him into such places, we will remain spiritually impoverished. We will never mature.

We can either make our fears work for us, or we can let them debilitate us. If we accept our fears, taking them to Christ, they will lead us into a more mature faith. But we will never run out of fears. There is always the smell of fear around the school of faith!

CONCLUSION

I HAVE A verse written on a card, sitting on my desk, that I review all the time. It is my personal prayer in this matter of fear. It reads, "I eagerly expect and hope that I will in no way be ashamed, but will have sufficient courage so that now as always Christ will be exalted in my body, whether by life or by death."[17] If I look within myself to find this courage, I won't find it. But when I look to the Holy Spirit for it, I am never disappointed.

Chapter 8

From Isolation to Freedom

* * *

My parents became Christians shortly before they were married. Over the next three years they set up a household, started a grocery business, and had the first two of an eventual six children: my older sister, Joann, and me.

They worked hard at everything they did, building their business, growing in their faith, and rearing their children. I memorized my first Bible verses standing on the toilet seat while my mother dressed me.

When I was nine, we moved from the small town of St. James, Minnesota, to Minneapolis. Dad wanted to further his education. As we settled into life in the big city we also settled into a small church where my parents immediately became actively involved. Living as Christians was the primary value in our household.

Because of this, I grew up with the feeling that I was different from the rest of my friends. We believed in Christ. Our family went to church. We had daily family devotions. Along with that, we lived with the inevitable list of prohibitions that churches like ours embraced at that time: no movies, no dancing, no card playing, and no smoking or drinking.

101

Maintaining a social life among my classmates while observing these rules proved to be awkward, especially in my teen years. Friendships could only go so far, and then I felt I had to draw back. If I accepted the party invitations, I knew I would face some awkward moments. There would be dancing—and probably some beer. It was easier to say no.

This, of course, kept me on the margins of much of the social life of my high school class. My friends thought I was aloof. But I saw no way out. I so respected my parents I never seriously considered going against them. Besides, one of the verses I had memorized standing on the toilet seat was, "Therefore come out from them and be separate, says the Lord. Touch no unclean thing."[1] That settled any argument I might have had. I made peace with the idea that Christians and nonChristians weren't supposed to be comfortable with each other.

I might have lived happily ever after, isolated in this peculiar little box of forbidden behaviors, had not my wife, Marge, and I moved to Brazil as missionaries. We went because of the gospel.

We elected to begin our ministry among university students. Being mostly Marxist in their orientation, they had rejected whatever ties they had had with the church. Obviously, if we wanted to connect with them, it would have to be on their turf. They showed no interest in our programs and were suspicious of our organization and its materials.

With no programs for us to run and no church to invite people to there was nowhere to hide. We found ourselves inescapably face to face with the people we had been sent to reach. My notions of how relationships between Christians and unbelievers worked were about to get hammered! Paul's words took on new significance for us. He said, "To the Jews I became like a Jew. . . . To those under the law I became like one under the law. . . . To those not having the law I became like one not having the law. . . . I have become all things to all men so that by all possible means I might save some. I do all this for the sake of the gospel."[2] According to Paul, the evangelist is to adapt to those he seeks to win. This was a new thought! Over the next years we learned what this really meant, a step at a time.

Lessons began in earnest the day I accepted an invitation to drop in on an acquaintance I had made on the street. When I arrived in his apartment he asked me what I wanted to drink. His options were gin or vodka. As he rushed out the door to purchase the Coke I had requested, the Holy Spirit reminded me, "If some unbeliever invites you to a meal and you want to go, eat whatever is put before you without raising questions of conscience."[3] It hit me that I wasn't getting it right with either God or people!

I learned to play *truco,* a Brazilian card game students love to play until 3:00 A.M. I learned what to yell at the referees at soccer matches, and I learned to cleanse my vocabulary of stained-glass words and to discuss the same great truths about God in street language. Over the years countless lessons of this sort led us into feeling increasingly at ease with our unbelieving friends, and them with us. We were learning to live as insiders.

THE PROBLEM OF LEGALISM . . .

BY THE TIME the first of our Brazilian friends had believed in Christ and had begun to grow in their faith, I had realized that my own notions of Christian behavior had less to do with the Bible than they did with the subculture in which I had been raised. It was obvious that I couldn't pass my scruples on. But then, I wondered, what should I give them? I began to comb the Scriptures. I was looking for truths to guide them into lifestyles that would honor Christ, that would be disciplined, and at the same time be attractive to their unbelieving friends. In short, we needed to help them avoid the trap of legalism.

I was surprised to discover how much space the New Testament devotes to this subject. If the importance of a truth can be measured in any fashion by the amount of attention Scripture gives it, then this one is really big! Legalism is a major issue in the Bible. It is there in the Gospels, in the center of the book of Acts, and numerous chapters in the Epistles address the subject as well.

. . . in the Gospels

In the Gospels, the phrase "Tradition of the elders" occurs repeatedly. This was a very specific, orally preserved set of rules and instructions that elaborated on the 613 laws of Moses. It spelled out in detail where the lines were between keeping and disobeying those laws. These rules told people what they could and couldn't do on the Sabbath, what constituted a tithe, what observances to keep and when to keep them—on and on until they controlled every aspect of daily life.

The Tradition of the elders was the flash point between Jesus and the scribes and Pharisees. (In the end the Jews justified his execution by those laws.) Jesus rejected them because they were a manmade set of rules being used as the official measurement of right and wrong. But they were a poor substitute for God's standard—especially as the Pharisees had figured out how to obey the letter of all those laws while at the same time living as they pleased! That's why Jesus called them hypocrites. He told them, "You shut the kingdom of heaven in men's faces. You yourselves do not enter, nor will you let those enter who are trying to."[4]

The Pharisees were legalists. That is, they attached human rules to God's Word and then treated both as having equal authority. Legalism is an obstacle to faith because it opposes grace, which is the heart of the gospel. Its rules become a false ladder to salvation.

. . . in the Book of Acts

The first major conflict in the early church revolved around this same issue of legalism. The church began as a movement among Jews. Then, in time, it spread into the surrounding nations, among the Gentiles. In Acts 13 we have the story of how Paul and Barnabas were sent out from the church in Antioch to take the gospel to the Gentiles. Their first missionary journey took them into the region of Galatia, where they preached the gospel the Holy Spirit had revealed to Paul—that is, "the Gentiles are heirs together with Israel, members together of one body,"[5] without having to go through Judaism to get there!

That message didn't sit well with some of the believers in Jerusalem. Being convinced their customs were an essential part of the gospel, several of them set out for Galatia to set the matter straight. They retraced the apostles' steps, making what they thought were the necessary amendments among the new believers.

Paul's reaction was immediate and crystal clear. He wrote, "If anybody is preaching to you a gospel other than what you accepted, let him be eternally condemned!"[6] Paul understood that anything added to the simple gospel of grace by faith would make it a nongospel.

This quickly became a full-blown conflict. The leaders of the entire church, both apostles and elders, met together in Jerusalem to work it out. The question was, What *is* required behavior for Gentile believers? Do they, or do they not, have to observe Jewish customs to be saved?

As the council opened, Paul and Barnabas were the first to speak. They described the fruit of God's workings among the Gentiles. Then Peter described what he had learned about the subject from his experience with Cornelius. James, the brother of Jesus, had the final word. He concluded, "We should not make it difficult for the Gentiles who are turning to God."[7] The decision was, Gentile believers would not be obligated to observe the Jewish customs. To do otherwise would be to add unnecessary burdens and make response to Christ more difficult.

Imagine what was at stake in this debate! What if it had gone the other way? If it had been decided that, yes, Gentile believers needed to submit to circumcision, observe Jewish customs, and keep the special days, the gospel would have been stopped in its tracks. It would have remained Jewish property, and we might not even have it today. The mobility of the gospel, its ability to move among the nations, was at stake in this debate.

. . . in the Epistles

The Epistles also give a lot of space to this matter of conduct and legalism. It is addressed in Romans 14; 1 Corinthians, chapters 8, 9, and 10; 2 Corinthians 6; the entire book of Galatians; Colossians, chapter 2; and Hebrews 5.

In the Gospels we saw that legalism is an obstacle to faith. In the book of Acts we saw it was an obstacle to the spreading of the gospel. Now, in the Epistles, legalism is identified as an obstacle to spiritual maturity. Paul put his finger on the connection between the two with the question, "Are you so foolish? After beginning with the Spirit, are you now trying to attain your goal by human effort?"[8] Legalistic rule-keeping is not the route to spiritual maturity. It is, instead, a cheap substitute for true spiritual maturity. It bypasses the deep work of transformation and settles, instead, for mere reformation or religious conformity.

Paul asked some believers in Colosse who had fallen into this trap, "Since you died with Christ . . . why . . . do you submit to . . . rules: 'Do not handle! Do not taste! Do not touch!'?" Then he explained the problem: "These are . . . based on human commands and teachings. Such regulations indeed have an appearance of wisdom . . . but they lack any value in restraining sensual indulgence."[9] One can keep all the rules, look really good to others, and at the same time be at war within one's self over his or her sensual desires. Legalistic rule-keeping is nothing more than a paint job that hides the real condition of the heart.

PURITY, MOBILITY, MATURITY

BEFORE GOING TO Brazil, I had not seen this. These three ideals—the purity of the gospel, its mobility in a society, and the maturing of those who believe in Christ (the very essence of everything we were seeking to accomplish)—were all put into jeopardy by this very subtle issue of legalism. I could see the threat against what we were seeking to do. We were working hard at making it clear that a relationship with Christ was available through grace and that nothing else at all could be added to that. Now the question, What is proper conduct? (What are the dos and don'ts of this Christian life?) threatened to alter this message. All we had to do was give people a list of acceptable and unacceptable behaviors, imposed upon us from some outside influence, and we would be on our way—headed in the wrong direction!

I had seen this happen in church-plants where the missionary had come to this point and had succumbed to the pressure to pass on a variation of the same list of behaviors I had grown up with. This resulted in the creation of a cultural enclave for those first believers. They appeared to be so odd in the eyes of their family and friends that the possibility of further spiritual generations was compromised. Walls of legalism cost them their access as insiders to their families and friends.

Another dimension to our understanding was added when Mario, who had just believed in Christ at that time, explained why, at the age of ten, he had left the church he had grown up in, resolved never to return. He felt the priest used fear to control and manipulate people. His message was, If you don't come to Mass and if you don't do your other religious duties you will perish in hades! Mario reacted against this use of fear and decided he would rather take his chances on his destiny.

Through that story and others that were similar, I understood that we were struggling with this issue of legalism on *both* sides; both the messenger and the receivers had legalisms to overcome in order for the gospel to run freely. This was a very crucial stage in our journey together. The purity of the message of grace, its future mobility among these new believers' families and friends, and the eventual spiritual maturity of all of us hung on how we would come out on this issue. We needed fresh answers from God!

Three Kinds of Behavior

SO WHAT DOES God want of us by way of lifestyle? The Scriptures identify three types of behavior. There are behaviors that are always right. There are some that are always wrong, and there are "disputable matters"[10]—matters that are right or wrong depending on the context.

Paul gives us a summary of behaviors that are always wrong. He writes, "The acts of the sinful nature are obvious: sexual immorality, impurity and debauchery; idolatry and witchcraft; hatred, discord, jealousy, fits of rage, selfish ambition, dissensions, factions and envy; drunkenness, orgies, and the like." He follows this with a description of behaviors that are always right; behaviors that fit everywhere, in whatever culture. These are "love, joy, peace, patience, kindness, goodness, faithfulness, gentleness and self control. Against such things," he says, "there is no law."[11]

Well, you ask, haven't we been talking about avoiding lists of behavior so people won't fall into legalism? What is this if it isn't just that—a list of approved and unapproved behaviors?

It is true. We could pin this list on our wall like a revised version of the Ten Commandments. Then we could set out to keep them. The results would be just as disastrous as they were with the first set of laws. We would utterly fail. That is the point of the gospel!

We need to look at the context of these paragraphs. Paul is not giving us a list to keep at all. He is describing what we can expect the Holy Spirit to do in us. He begins the paragraph with these words: "So I say, live by the Spirit, and you will not gratify the desires of the sinful nature." Then as he gets into the "right" behaviors, he prefaces his description by calling them "the fruit of the Spirit."[12]

There is a world of difference between submitting to the Holy Spirit and submitting to human regulations. Fruit of the Spirit comes from him! It is the outworking of his inner workings in us. The effects on those who are watching are equally distinct. True transformation from within baffles those who know us best. They can't believe we've actually changed. The wonder of it draws the observer to look more closely. But when our religion comes across as being a set of rules we are following and trying to impose on others, people flee!

Some behaviors are always right. Others are always wrong. That's clear. Now, what about "disputable matters"?

Paul used this term "disputable matters" to refer to questions of behavior not specifically addressed in Scripture. One of these in Paul's day was going into the pagan temple and eating food that had been offered to idols. The list of disputable matters shifts constantly as our culture changes. Over the centuries everything from wearing colored clothing to sleeping on a soft bed has had its turn on the list. When we look back, yesterday's list of disputable matters always seems so quaint, such as those I grew up with fifty years ago. It also seems people defend their lists with exaggerated zeal. It's as if they were defending the faith itself!

How easy it is to fall into heated arguments over questions of conduct! Why do we do that? I think it is because it is human nature to train one's conscience to respond according to one's beliefs. Matters of conscience, by definition, run deep. We get emotional about them. So, in these doubtful matters we not only have our own consciences to deal with, we have the other person's conscience to worry about as well! The Bible says, "Do not cause anyone to stumble, whether Jews, Greeks or the church of God."[13] People stumble when they are prompted to act in a way that violates their consciences.

In that case, you say, we're stuck! I'm told not to violate my own conscience. And I am told to care about other people's consciences as well. Certainly someone, somewhere, is going to have a conscience against whatever I do. I know if I join my unbelieving friends on their turf, I will offend some of my Christian friends. But I also know that if I let their consciences determine my behavior, I won't even have nonChristian friends. That's where I was stuck as a teen, and that's where many people who have it in their hearts to live as insiders are stuck. How do we sort this out?

TWO LAWS

THE BIBLE IDENTIFIES two laws, or principles, that will guide us in our deciding what to do when we are confronted with a decision over a doubtful matter. The two laws are the law of love and the law of self-control.

The Law of Love

Paul stated this law in his letter to the Romans. He wrote, "He who loves his fellowman has fulfilled the law. The commandments . . . are summed up in this one rule: 'Love your neighbor as yourself.' Love does no harm to its neighbor. Therefore love is the fulfillment of the law."[14]

How do we decide on a disputable matter? According to this verse it looks obvious! All I need to do is ask myself, How, in this situation, do I show love to this person? When I do that, I can assume I have made the right choice. And I'll get it right, most of the time, but not always. There is another consideration: I also have to ask, Can I, personally, handle this choice? We need to observe the law of self-control as well.

The Law of Self-control

David has been following Christ for about six months. He began to think about God while he was in a twelve-step program for drug abusers. As he prayed to the "higher power," he wondered about God. He wondered if he really existed and, if so, what he was like. When he joined our little Bible study in an office complex he seemed to recognize Jesus at first sight. David's life had been wrecked by his addiction and by several bad choices, but the healing that is now taking place is written all over his face!

Recently, David announced that he is determined not to go back to hang out with his old friends. Instead, he is moving in the other direction, breaking his ties with his old network. He finds this difficult and painful—but necessary. He's obeying the "law of self-control." This law says, "'Everything is permissible for me'—but not everything is beneficial. 'Everything is permissible for me'—but I will not be mastered by anything."[15] He would risk temptations he would not be able to handle if he set out to be an insider among the people in his old haunts.

The gospel is the good news about freedom. "It is for freedom that Christ has set us free," Paul writes. "Stand firm, then, and do not let yourselves be burdened again by a yoke of slavery."[16] David doesn't want to even get close to his old "yoke of slavery," for fear he might end up wearing it again.

These two laws—the law of love and of self-control—take us further down the road toward freedom in Christ. We pursue this freedom because we will not grow into spiritual maturity without it. And we pursue it for the sake of the people among whom we are an insider. We need to be free to bring them into our life and to participate in theirs.

FOUR KINDS OF PEOPLE

WE HAVE MADE progress in sorting through our questions on conduct and legalism. We can see the road up ahead, but we're still not quite out of the woods. It still looks like we are going to offend some people, no matter how good our choices are. That is often the case. So we must ask one final question before we draw our conclusions: What do I do when I find I can't please everyone?

It has been helpful for me to understand that there are four kinds of people I need to keep in mind as I go along. They are mature believers, unbelievers, new believers, and weak believers.

1. Mature Believers

Mature believers are the ones we least worry about. They know "no food is unclean in itself," that "the kingdom of God is not a matter of eating and drinking."[17] They aren't offended by these questions of conscience.

2. Unbelievers

The second group is unbelievers. They have priority. Paul adapted his lifestyle to the people he was seeking to reach. He said, "I have become all things to all men so that by all possible means I might save some."[18] Sometimes it's tempting to treat this priority as the final word and just forget about everyone else. That would simplify a lot of things. But we can't do that, as we shall see.

3. New Believers

New believers are the third group. They are recent transfers from the dominion of Satan into the kingdom of God.[19] They too have priority. They come broken because they've spent their lives crashing around in the darkness. Their lives are marked by broken relationships and broken hopes. Now they face the challenge of breaking their codependencies and addictions. This is the person Paul is talking about when he warns, "We who are strong ought to bear with the failings of the weak and not to please ourselves."[20] He is talking about people like David.

New believers of the first century had to pick their way out of an idolatry that involved sacrifices to the gods, temple prostitution, and demon worship. They were still weak, still vulnerable, still sorting through the differences between the old life and the new. Paul is saying, Respect that! Don't just think about yourselves; think about helping these new believers move back away from the edge and along toward maturity.

4. Weak Believers

The chronically weak believer is our fourth consideration. These people are weak in a way new believers are not. They are spiritual dwarfs. The writer of the book of Hebrews tells them that "though by this time you ought to be teachers, you need someone to teach you the elementary truths of God's word all over again. You need milk, not solid food!"[21]

The chronically weak, the writer explains, never quite get the foundations of their faith laid. Grace is not clear. Neither is God's forgiveness. Consequently, they never get around to figuring out what is good and what is evil. They are legalists. The writer continues, Let us "go on to maturity, not laying again the foundation of repentance . . . and of faith in God."[22] Where faith is not the foundation, the only thing left for the religious person is to invent and follow rules. That becomes his or her version of spiritual maturity.

One of the things that makes this discussion on freedom and conduct so difficult is that we have so many chronically weak people in our churches today. They intimidate us with their threats of taking offense! At these times, we think of what Jesus said will happen to a person who offends another. We can just feel the millstone around our neck. So we back away.

We need to understand that the chronically weak are not fragile in the way the new believer is. These people have been around for a while and have settled into a legalistic lifestyle they are not about to abandon. You won't likely cause them to stumble. But they will judge you when you deviate from their notion of right and wrong. We can't allow the fear of being judged to control what we do. If we did, we would never be able to obey Christ. When we are judged, we turn that over to God, who *is* the judge and will judge us all. Judging another is, in itself, sin.

"USE YOUR FREEDOM . . . TO . . . SERVE."[23]

I GREW UP within the walls of the church. I don't resent this, nor do I blame anyone for it. It's the way things work. Every group of people who seek to create a shared identity will, with time, create its own unique code of conduct. Keeping the code is an act of belonging. It's tribalism. Every group will have its own tribal smell, whether it is a gang of bikers or a congregation of Baptists. Behave in a certain way and you're in. Everybody else is an outsider! The code creates walls between "us and them." As an insider, we need to understand how this works—and not get stuck behind the walls.

So what about my standing-on-the-toilet-seat verse: "Come out from among them and be separate"? What do I do with that? Somewhere along the line I had to learn that being separate isn't a matter of geography—where I might be physically. It is a question of who has my heart and mind. In praying for his disciples, Jesus said, "I will remain in the world no longer, but they are still in the world. . . . My prayer is not that you take them out of the world but that you protect them from the evil one. . . . Sanctify them by the truth; your word is truth. As you sent me into the world, I have sent them into the world."[24]

If the Spirit of God has my heart, and the Word of God has my mind, I can go anywhere and be with anyone. I am still "separate"!

CHAPTER 9

But How Will I Find the Time?

* * *

From the movie *The Matrix:*

> Morpheus: "Let me tell you why you're here. You're here
> because you know something. What you know you can't
> explain. But you feel it. You've felt it all your life. There is
> something wrong with the world. You don't know what it is,
> but it's there—like a splinter in your mind. It's driving you
> mad. It's this feeling that brought you to me. Do you know
> what I'm talking about?"
>
> Neo: "The Matrix."
>
> Morpheus: "Do you want to know what it is? The Matrix is
> everywhere. It is all around us. It is there when you look
> out your window, when you turn on your television. You
> feel it when you go to work, when you're in church, when
> you pay your taxes. It's a world that's being pulled over
> your eyes to blind you from the truth."
>
> Neo: "What truth?"

Morpheus: "That you're a slave, Neo. Like everyone else, you've
been born into bondage: a bondage you cannot smell or
taste; a prison for your mind."[1]

Recently, Mike spent a weekend in Minneapolis with a group
of people, interacting over many of the things we are talking
about in this book. The group had come together because
they were motivated by the idea of living and ministering as insiders. They
wanted help in making it happen. But all of them, in one way or another,
asked the same question: Where will I find the time?

All of their stories were similar. Both husband and wife worked.
They spent Saturdays transporting the kids to their team sports and
music lessons. On Sunday they went to church—and then watched the
Vikings. Then it was back to work. In summary they were saying, We
don't have the time or energy to spend with people in this way.

This is not unusual. Mike and I hear similar stories wherever we
travel. It is probably your story as well. To one degree or another it's
the story of all of us. As the information revolution takes over, time has
become our most valued commodity. It is scarcer than money.

Today, women are working an average of 41.7 hours per week, while
men are working 48.8 hours. Because two-thirds of women work outside
the home, the median husband-wife unit is putting in 90 hours a week
on the job.[2] Our technology puts further burdens on what remains of our
time. Recently the *Wall Street Journal* ran a full-page ad that simply read,
"The good news is, you are always connected to the office. The bad news
is, you are always connected to the office."[3]

What happened? We thought we were in control; but here we are,
totally absorbed by our busy yet increasingly isolated life!

And now we're talking about living as an *insider!* How is that going to
work? We will not find space for this by tinkering with our priorities, or

by honing our time-management skills a bit more. The issue is much deeper than that. As Morpheus told Neo, we are "in a bondage you cannot smell or taste; a prison for your mind."[4]

We find ourselves caught in a lifestyle that consumes both our time and attention. Yet, Christ lives in our heart. Every day he calls us afresh to walk with him. Our deepest desire is to do just that, but we are quickly distracted by the multitude of other voices in our ears. We don't know how to handle the inner conflict that stems from this. Some of us have just given up, shutting our ears to him. It's just too painful. We didn't want this to happen to us, but we don't know what else to do. We can hardly resign from the responsibilities of everyday life!

What do we do? That's the subject of this chapter. In this chapter we will discuss three questions. Hopefully, they will give us the perspective we need to find our way to freedom. The questions are: (1) What has happened to our society that puts us in this situation today? (2) What are the effects of modernity upon us? and (3) How do we reorient ourselves to live as an insider?

WHAT HAPPENED TO OUR SOCIETY?

OVER THE PAST five hundred years, from medieval times until today, Western society has gone through a series of revolutions that have transformed our world, both in the way we live and in the way we think.

Religion ruled in medieval society. Truth was determined theologically, and much of what was on people's minds revolved around the afterlife. However, those were not "the good old days," as the dogmas of the church were imposed arbitrarily on people. Fear was a controlling factor in everyday life.

Things began to change with the contributions of several very unusual people whose influences converged in a thirty-year period, between 1490 and 1520. Some of these were Copernicus (1473–1543), who introduced a new cosmology; Michelangelo (1475–1564), who with his art proclaimed a new man; Christopher Columbus (1451–1506), who discovered a new world; and Martin Luther (1483–1546), who contributed to the breakup of the monolithic structure of the Roman Catholic Church.

They were part of the Renaissance, or "rebirth," of Western civilization. The idea of the Renaissance was to recover the culture of the Greek and Roman eras. It was a rebirth of interest in nature, knowledge, beauty, and creativity. Several technical inventions, like the magnetic compass and the printing press, helped propel society forward into the modern era.

The Enlightenment, or Age of Reason (which began in the mid-seventeenth century), inevitably followed. Faith in the power of human reason was the driving idea of this period. With advances in knowledge such as Isaac Newton's (1642–1727) startling insight that the earth and planets are controlled by gravity, and Francis Bacon's (1561–1626) articulation of the scientific method, society moved from a religious to a humanistic worldview. We placed our faith in ourselves. Equipped with the tools of science and confident in the power of our reason, we were convinced we would build a saner, more humane world. Science became our new oracle. Only the unbiased analysis of data was admissible in our search for truth.

The Enlightenment gave rise not only to a scientific revolution but to a philosophical revolution as well. Copernicus, with his new cosmology, had convinced us that the earth is not the center of the universe. Charles Darwin (1809–1892) published his conclusion that the human being is just one more beast, evolved through time and chance. And Sigmund Freud (1856–1939) argued that even our best, most well-reasoned arguments are cover-ups for our irrational, bestial impulses. The cumulative effect of these and other related observations led us, eventually, into an unsettling conclusion: that the human mind cannot be relied upon to accurately judge reality. So, even as some were proclaiming the sovereignty of human reason, the seeds that would debunk the idea were being sown by others.

This conclusion—that there is no metastory, no big truth that ties all the pieces together—gained momentum early in the twentieth century. It has carried the West into what is called postmodernism. We are post-modern in that we have now rejected both biblical religion and modern science as sources for truth. *Truth* has become whatever works for the individual. According to this doctrine, there are no absolutes.

Meanwhile, as these ideas were growing in our minds, we were busy applying our new science and technology in our factories and in the marketplace. We discovered that a factory, plus raw materials, plus labor can produce wealth. We learned how to manufacture using interchange-able parts and how to run an assembly line. We learned to mass-produce goods. Then we learned how to market this production. Production and marketing became a new source of wealth, one that was not dependent upon owning land, as it was in the Middle Ages. We had created the Industrial Revolution.*

The key figure in this revolution was the consumer, without whom this new economy would be dead. As Charles Kettering, once head of General Motors, said, "The key to economic prosperity is the organized creation of dissatisfaction."[5] So, we deliberately created the consumer.

Industry embarked on a deliberate crusade to convert the American from the traditional values of Yankee frugality and frontier self-sacrifice to consumerism. Culture critic Jeremy Rifkin put it as follows:

> The mass consumption phenomenon did not occur sponta-
> neously, nor was it the inevitable by-product of an insatiable
> human nature. Quite the contrary. Economists at the turn of the

---

*Began in Great Britain during the 1700s and spread to North America in the early 1800s.

century noted that most working people were content to earn just enough income to provide for their basic needs and a few luxuries, after which they preferred increased leisure time over additional work hours and extra income. . . . The fact that people preferred to trade additional hours of work for additional hours of leisure time became a critical concern and a bane to businessmen whose inventories of goods were quickly piling up on factory floors and in warehouses across the nation.[6]

Marketing was born. The ideas of fashion, of being in vogue or "chic," were introduced. Brand names began to appear, and planned obsolescence helped keep it all moving.

In the 1950s the commercial jet, television, and the advent of the computer began to shrink our world. Since 1985 satellites, fax machines, personal computers, cell phones, and pagers have turned our globe into a single, virtual office. We are in the midst of an information revolution. Information about anything, everywhere, is at our fingertips. Our world today is very small indeed.

WHAT ARE THE EFFECTS OF MODERNITY UPON US?

THE WORD *MODERNITY* is defined by this process we just described. Modernity is a world system built upon the foundation of science and technology, and it depends upon a market economy. "Progress" is inherent to the idea of modernity, and economic growth has become its measurement.

The science and technology that drive modernity have brought us countless benefits. Machines multiply the effects of our labor, modern medicine heals our body, and our table is filled with foods that only technology could bring us. Virtually every area of life has been enhanced by our modern way of doing things. No one would want to return to the short, brutish existence that preceded what we have today. But modernity has come with a price.

The impact of these revolutions in science, technology, and economics, combined with what they have done to the way we think, has left us reeling. The driving values of science (knowing more), technology (doing more), and economics (having more) are relentless. We scramble in our personal life to keep up. To do so, we have opted to outsource many of the things most important to us. Childrearing is outsourced to daycare, conversation is outsourced to the therapist or counselor, recreation to the Little League teams, and grandmother to the assisted care facility. We no longer dine. We eat—at the fast-food restaurant. Whatever is left of our time and energy has been shrink-wrapped by our cell phone and PC. They suck out whatever free space remains in our agenda. Nobody is at home anymore because nothing happens there.

LIES WE LIVE BY

IN ONE OF Jesus' many confrontations with the Pharisees, he asked a rhetorical question—and then answered it himself. He asked, "Why is my language not clear to you?"

Then he answered, It is "because you are unable to hear what I say. You belong to your father, the devil, and you want to carry out your father's desire . . . for there is no truth in him. When he lies, he speaks his native language, for he is a liar and the father of lies."[7]

One thing we can count on, with Satan being the "prince of this world"[8] much of what we sincerely believe in, as a society, is actually false! Along the way, over these five hundred years briefly reviewed here, we have picked up one lie here, another there—and they have become a part of the foundation of our culture. They are with us today as unchallenged assumptions and are taking our society in some deadly directions.

As followers of Christ, we are not immune to the power of these lies. We can embrace them as unthinkingly as everyone else does. They are there, lodged in our mind. We need to submit our heart to God's Spirit and his Word, in order to first identify them, and then to tear down "barriers erected against the truth of God, [and to fit] every loose thought and emotion and impulse into the structure of life shaped by Christ."[9]

Two such lies (there are many) are especially relevant to the subject of this chapter. They are the source of much of the pressure we have been describing. They were planted in our souls almost two centuries ago and have warred against us ever since. They are, first, the idea that "progress is knowing more, doing more, and having more"[10]; and second, the notion that "liberty consists in doing what one desires."[11]

"Progress is knowing more, doing more, and having more."

This is one of the seminal ideas of the Enlightenment. But because progress has proven so difficult to define, we have dumbed down our definition to where we can claim some success. Rather than asking if peace on earth and good will toward mankind is making any headway, we merely quantify whatever we are doing. We measure its size. We have told ourselves that "big is good, bigger is better, and biggest is best." This criterion is applied everywhere—to business, to churches, to our investment portfolios, on and on. Even the houses we live in make the statement. Americans have doubled the square footage of their homes over the past forty years—while the size of our families has become smaller.[12]

This inevitably leads to the idea that "you are what you own." Rather than recognizing a person for his or her character or achievement, we award status to people on the basis of what they can buy.

This whole cluster of lies has to do with consumerism in one way or another. All of them reflect the falsehood that says, "I will be happier when I get more of whatever I'm after." Whenever we're tempted to doubt this idea, the next billboard or TV commercial will be there to reassure us that being a consumer is the road to the good life.

Now we're caught. The time will come when our society will have to harvest the fruit of this lie. We cannot abandon our consuming because if we do the economy will fold. So, whether we want or need the stuff or not, we must keep buying it. And that means keeping up the helter-skelter pace to earn the money for our purchases. The consumer is being consumed by the product.

> "A deluded heart misleads him;
> he cannot save himself, or say,
> 'Is not this thing in my right hand a lie?'"[13]

"Liberty consists in doing what one desires."

The American Declaration of Independence defends the rights to "life, liberty, and the pursuit of happiness." John Stuart Mill, in his 1859 treatise *On Liberty,* carried this idea of rights one step further when he penned the statement, "Liberty consists in doing what one desires." This notion of rights has become another false idea that exerts an enormous influence upon us.

Wars have been fought to defend the freedoms that declaration describes. But now postmodernity, with its rejection of both biblical religion and modern science as foundations for truth, has opened the way for an interpretation of those rights that threatens to tear the fabric of the nation.

Divested of any metastory, the Bill of Rights is being used as a manifesto against any restraint on the individual. John Stuart Mill called for a freedom for the individual "where conduct that merely concerns himself, his independence, is, of right, absolute." He maintained that the individual is to be "free of constraints imposed by religion, morality, law, family and community."[14]

This expresses a very one-sided notion of freedom. Freedom cannot exist without discipline. I have no freedom to express myself musically on the piano because I haven't submitted to the discipline of practicing on the instrument. In the same way, values that revolve only around the self soon rob us of the very things we aspire to. They leave us incapable of even maintaining an enduring relationship with another person as they work against our committing to anyone but ourselves.

So, today's pop wisdom leaves us with some deadly slogans:

"You owe it to yourself to achieve your full potential."

"If this relationship isn't good for me, I'm out of here."

Both of these are lies—at best, half-truths. It's a road that leads not to freedom and self-fulfillment as is advertised, but to personal isolation. Our life has become so individualistic that we no longer think in terms of teaming up even as a family to move together toward a common vision. We live in hot pursuit of our own fulfillment. Consequently, we can't stay married. We can't pry our fingers off the rungs of the ladder to career success, and we can't raise our children. They are left to be reared by people who make that, literally, their business.

What more has to happen before we admit something is fundamentally wrong with our way of life?

Reorienting Ourselves to Live As Insiders

"Don't become so well adjusted to your culture that you fit into it without even thinking."[15]

IT IS OUR pursuit of lies, such as the two we've addressed here, that keeps us on the run, robbing us of our life. We don't take the time to stop and think about it, but we have joined the stampede in pursuit of consumption and personal fulfillment at the expense of everything else. This pursuit is so absorbing it eclipses others that are nobler, such as living as an insider.

I am not suggesting we give away our laptop and cell phone and go live in a tree someplace. There are times when that might sound pretty good, but we cannot abandon our place in society. Remember, we are called to live as an insider within it. We make significant progress toward freedom, however, just by identifying the lies we live by. When we see them for what they are, they no longer have control over us. They can drive us no longer. We need to remember that, before anything else, we are citizens of the kingdom of God. He calls us to align our notions of progress and success accordingly. Understanding this alone will change a lot of things.

We are beginning to understand that being an insider isn't about adding one more activity to an already frantic life. We're not just talking about finding the time, or making some space in our schedule for some additional activities. It's more than that. This calls for a change in paradigms—a full-scale reorienting of our mind. It means operating on a different set of values—a departure from the mindless rush to keep up, to walking in tune with God's purposes. It is replacing one way of life with another. (We'll develop this idea further in chapter 18.)

IT'S TIME TO TAKE THINGS BACK

IN THE MEANTIME, there are things we can do immediately to reclaim parts of our life we never should have let go of in the first place. We have outsourced our life away! Now, we need to take certain things back!

Prior to the Industrial Revolution, most people's lives revolved around a single axis: the *home*. Goods were manufactured in "cottage industries"—usually in sheds attached to the house or barn. Everyone in the family had something to do, and the family, together with perhaps a couple of other hired workers, made the whole thing go. Children went off to school every day, and on Sundays everyone went to church together. Life was lived within a single, cohesive social network.

The society in which the church was birthed was even more integrated. The basic unit of the society was the *household*. A household consisted of the extended family—plus a few other people who served as artisans, tutors, and whatever else was needed. The household was headed by the patriarch—or matriarch—of the family, and each was pretty much an economic "ecosystem" on its own. The root of our word *economy* is derived from the Greek word *oikos* or "household." A reading of the New Testament, with its constant referral to households, reveals that this was where the church lived its life as well. In fact, the household served as the primary form for the church during the first three hundred years of its history. There were virtually no church buildings.

Think of it! When you were at home you were everywhere you needed to be. You were at work, at school, in church, at leisure—and at home, all at the same time. Today, separate institutions perform each of these functions. Each involves a separate set of people who often share nothing else in common with the others. We can live a busy life where we are surrounded by people all day, every day, and still live in isolation.

We can do something about this. We must do something about it if we hope to stop dissipating our life. We have let society put activities over people in our value system, and we are unquestioningly going along for the ride. *That's just the way life is*, we reason.

Not really! It is more accurate to say that's how we've chosen to live. We have chosen to just go along for the ride.

DRAW A PICTURE OF YOUR LIFE

STOP! TAKE AN hour and draw a picture of your life. Draw in your family, your work, your social life, your church, school, Little League, lessons, exercise routines, and so on. Look it all over. Now, write in the names of the people you connect with in each of these activities. Highlight the names of the people who especially matter to you. Begin to see those people as your "household."

How does it look? What does this tell you about your life? Is it too insular? Is it too dispersed? Where are you headed?

If we hope to stop letting life run us, we must make choices. Ask yourself, Who, and what, is important to me? Who, and what, gets my time and attention? Once we've answered those questions, we have criteria by which we can say yes or no to the demands that come along. We can *focus* our time and attention. When we've refocused our life we will have taken a big part of it back.

CHAPTER 10

OUR PERSONAL INADEQUACIES

* * *

We have looked at three obstacles that threaten our ability to live as an insider. They are our fears, our scruples, and our busy-ness. One more obstacle remains that will, if not confronted, surely take us out of the picture. It is our feelings of personal inadequacy. Those can come from any number of sources.

We look at what's going on in our life and think, *How would God ever use me with other people when my own life falls so far short? How can I tell people about "peace with God" when I worry about my job, our finances, and the company my kids are keeping? Who am I to say anything to anybody?*

Others feel disqualified because of a relationship that has gone bad. They may be working through some deep struggles in their marriages. They may be feeling powerless as they try to recover from recent divorces. Many have heartaches with children and conflicts with the extended family; or they have made some enemies at work. We feel guilty about relational difficulties such as these—we feel like failures, like people who don't have the right to say anything to anybody.

Sometimes it is true. Sometimes we *do* fail. We *do* lose credibility! The most common objection to the gospel I hear from people in business has to do with bad business experiences they have had with people who identify themselves as Christians. It's as the apostle Paul pointed out: "God's name is blasphemed among the Gentiles because of you."[1]

It *is* possible to discredit the gospel by the way we live. But this doesn't happen as often as we may think or for the reasons we might imagine. Most often our feelings of inadequacy are rooted in one more of those lies Satan feeds us to keep us under his control. We hear him say, Real Christians don't have problems. They don't mess up—and you do! Sort out your own life before you try to be of help to anyone else. We listen to this, and keep quiet.

But let us suppose it is true! Let us suppose I have, in fact, discredited my testimony, that the news is out that I've been dishonest in my business dealings. What am I going to do about that? Am I going to leave it that way and just sit it out for the rest of my life? Or am I going to step into the light and get beyond it? Healing comes as we are honest, first before God, and then before others. Whether we have, in fact, lost credibility or whether our feelings of inadequacy are of our own fabrication, the best possible environment for spiritual progress is one in which we are engaged with God in the lives of other people. When we are, we will find that even our weaknesses can be used by God for our benefit and for others.

Mike's Story

FOR MANY YEARS my life was based on two false assumptions: First, I believed I had to achieve a certain level of competence and have my life together before God could use me—and that I wasn't quite there yet. I also had the idea that if I were transparent and let people see my weaknesses and struggles, it would invalidate what I had to say about Christ. As you can imagine, this combination produced feelings of guilt, anxiety, and deep inner dissatisfaction.

I didn't get these ideas from the Scriptures. They came out of my childhood. Some of my earliest memories of my father are of him leaving on yet another trip. His work as a political strategist and organizer required him to be absent for long periods of time. This left my mother at home with two small boys. I was the oldest. Mother struggled with bouts of severe depression, so we never knew what a day would hold for us. Would she be up or would she be down?

As a young boy I searched for security. I craved stability and certainty. I soon discovered that whenever I performed competently, I would gain my parents' praise. For a boy living in a world of an absentee father and a mother who struggled to cope, this praise was the closest I could get to the real love and acceptance I longed for. Performance became my way of controlling my uncertain life.

I carried this pattern into my adult life and into my faith in Christ. I was uncomfortable in situations I couldn't control. That being the case, faith, by its very definition, posed a special problem for me. "Faith is being . . . certain of what we do not see."[2] In other words, it isn't really faith until we get beyond what we can control! That was a frightening idea for me. I feared that if I followed God into where he wanted to lead me, my incompetence would be exposed and I would be seen as a failure. I found it hard to open my hand on my need to control my world and respond to God's call to follow him by faith.

Over the years, God has gradually delivered me from these deeply entrenched patterns that held me prisoner. One of the Scriptures the Holy Spirit used most to free me is the second letter Paul wrote to the believers in Corinth. Here's what I saw.

A Man Under Attack

PAUL'S CREDIBILITY WAS under attack when he wrote this second letter to the Christians in Corinth. Certain people were attempting to discredit his legitimacy as an apostle and minister of the gospel. They were trying to undermine his influence in order to draw the Corinthian believers into their own orbit of influence. They were false teachers!

Paul's previous letter had been quite confrontational. In it he dealt with several hard situations within the church, such as quarrels, sexual immorality, lawsuits, and some chaos. In this second letter to the Corinthians, we find Paul concerned for how his previous letter had been received. He was also concerned about how some people seemed to be misinterpreting his failure to visit them as he had planned. Apparently some people were using those things—the hard letter and the aborted trip—to create dissent and undermine Paul's authority. They were saying, Paul doesn't really love you. Look at this letter he wrote! And then he didn't even show up when he told you he would. He can't be a real apostle. True apostles don't do things like that. You need to follow us. We have better credentials for leadership than he does.

Paul knew all about these goings-on when he wrote this letter. He knew there were people trying to take over and that they were using questions about his credentials as leverage. They were demanding proof of Paul's legitimacy as an apostle. He hated that sort of thing, as making one's credentials public is, more often than not, little more than a sophisticated form of boasting. But he chose to play their little game. He knew it would provide the setting for teaching his spiritual children one of the greatest truths of the Christian life.

THE GAME

BEFORE HE STARTED the game, this bit of madness, he had one thing
to say to his spiritual children. He wanted them to know the truth about
him. So he wrote, in effect, There is only one credential that can validate
my ministry among you, and I have that credential. You're it! "You yourselves are our letter, written on our hearts . . . written not with ink but
with the Spirit of the living God."[3] Each of you, every one of your names,
is right here written on my heart, Paul says. You know that, and so do I.
That's my credential—the only one I really need to defend my ministry
among you. If that is clear, then this whole silly debate is a nonevent.

With that, Paul made his first moves in the game of one-upmanship.
If they wanted to boast, he could match them boast for boast.

What anyone dares to boast about—I am speaking as a fool—I
also dare to boast about.

Are they Hebrews? So am I.
Are they Israelites? So am I.
Are they Abraham's descendents? So am I.

Are they servants of Christ? (I am out of my mind to talk like
this.) I am more. I have worked much harder, been in prison more
frequently, been flogged more severely . . . exposed to death again
and again. . . . I received from the Jews the forty lashes minus
one. . . . I was beaten . . . stoned . . . shipwrecked. . . . I have been
. . . in danger from bandits . . . from my own countrymen . . . in
danger in the city . . . the country . . . at sea . . . from false brothers.
I have known hunger . . . thirst . . . I have been cold and naked.

Besides everything else, I face daily the pressure of my concern for all the churches.[4]

Now, while we're in this pointless, boasting mode, Paul continues, Let me tell you what I'm really proud of! "If I must boast, I will boast of the things that show my weakness."[5]

THE GREAT PARADOX

HIS WEAKNESSES! HERE is a man whose credibility is under attack. He has been asked to submit his credentials. His spiritual children are wondering how he will measure up—and what will become of them after it's all over. And Paul starts talking about his personal weaknesses! That would be like your being on the short-list for an important job. It's down to you and three others. Then you go in for the deciding interview with the selecting panel. In the interview, instead of talking about the great things you will bring to the company if they employ you, you describe your past failures.

The failure Paul chose to talk about went way back to an incident that happened at the very beginning of his ministry. It was his very first attempt to preach about Christ. It happened in Damascus right after his conversion. He reminded the Corinthians of how "the governor under King Aretas had the city . . . guarded in order to arrest me. But I was lowered in a basket from a window in the wall and slipped through his hands."[6] What did that event have to do with this subject of Paul's weaknesses? We need to go to the account of the story in the book of Acts to get the answer.

The record of the event in the book of Acts shows that immediately after Paul's conversion "he began to preach in the synagogues that Jesus is the Son of God. All those who heard him were astonished and asked, 'Isn't he the man who raised havoc in Jerusalem among those who call on this name?' . . . Yet Saul grew more and more powerful and baffled the

Jews living in Damascus by proving that Jesus is the Christ."[7]

That's a failure, we ask? He overpowered and baffled his opponents! He was able to prove to the Jews that Jesus is the Christ. That sounds like success! The next verse explains it: "After many days had gone by, the Jews conspired to kill him. . . . But his followers took him by night and lowered him in a basket through an opening in the wall."[8] The goal is not to win the argument. It is to help people see Jesus. Instead of people turning to Christ as a result of his powerful persuasion, he had to run for his life—in the basket normally used for garbage disposal.

From Damascus, Paul went to Jerusalem where he tried the same thing again, "speaking boldly in the name of the Lord. He talked and debated with the Grecian Jews," and the same thing happened. The text continues, "but they tried to kill him." This new convert was becoming more trouble than he was worth, so, "When the brothers [in Jerusalem] learned of this, they . . . sent him off to Tarsus."[9] They had to get him out of there. Paul spent his next years in Tarsus and Arabia until Barnabas went and found him and brought him to Antioch to help with the church there.

These first attempts by the apostle Paul that ended in failure were watershed events for him. Isn't it interesting that, out of all his rich experiences over the years, he looks back and singles out that failure in Damascus as being among the very most important of his life? It was important because it taught him a major lesson.

Look at the difference between the brashly aggressive man who confronted the Jews in Damascus and the man who took the gospel to the people in Corinth. Paul writes, "I came to you in weakness and fear, and with much trembling. My message and my preaching were not with wise and persuasive words, but with a demonstration of the Spirit's power."

This time Paul came in weakness! Not that he wasn't capable of being more assertive. He had started out that way, with all the forcefulness in the world—and discovered it to be fruitless. Paul consciously discarded that approach for another, more powerful way. He chose to live under submission to the Holy Spirit. Why? "So that your faith might not rest on man's wisdom, but on God's power."[10] He was looking for enduring, eternal results.

As we go through our daily routine, we will either depend upon ourselves, or upon God. In a sense, it is easier, less stressful, to live life in our own way, trusting in ourselves. It gives us the illusion that we are in control. We know our stuff. We are prepared, and so we take on the world.

Trusting the Holy Spirit, on the other hand, can be unsettling! With him in the lead we are never sure how whatever we are doing is going to turn out. We will still prepare ourselves to do our work, but we know his intentions might at times be different from ours. On occasion, he might even decide to let us look like failures. We don't like to live like that, and we probably won't until after we, too, have had a couple rides in the garbage basket.

That's why we need our inadequacies. Without them we will never understand our need for true strength. It is difficult for us to embrace the paradox: that in Christ, we are weak when we think we are strong, and strong when we know we are weak. Spiritual fruitfulness does not come out of our feeling strong and self-assured. Spiritual fruit can only come from the Holy Spirit.

Embracing Our Hardships, Weaknesses, and Difficulties

The weakness of God is stronger that man's strength. . . . Not many of you were wise by human standards; not many were influential; not many were of noble birth. But God chose the foolish things of the world to shame the wise; God chose the weak things of the world to shame the strong.[11]

IT IS NOT easy for us to face up to our inadequacies, but our life will be sterile in the areas where it matters most until we do. We often miss this fact. We think we're getting by and looking good on our own, but there will be no enduring fruit until we awaken to our true weakness.

Mike continues . . .

Audrey and I have spent our last thirty years in and out of the school of faith. The curriculum seems to consist primarily of experiences that reveal to us our inadequacies and show us our need to depend upon God. The first course we went through was unforgettable. It lasted about three years, between October 1975 and May 1978.

During that period, my father, at age forty-nine, died from a heart attack, and my mother, consumed with grief, fell into a deep depression. She became angry and irrationally demanding. In February 1976, our first child was born. Then, at the end of that year, we moved to another city where I had taken a teaching job. Our second daughter was born in 1977, and nearly died five months later. Money was scarce. I realized I couldn't control this situation no matter how hard I tried to perform. As my self-sufficiency ran out, feelings of desperation took over. We began to look to God, and he was there to meet us.

Now, years later as we look back, we are thankful for the priceless lessons we began to learn in that period. They have guided us ever since. We learned it is not the hardship in itself that helps us know God better. It is when we embrace the hardship by faith, seeing it as an opportunity to experience God's power, that we grow toward maturity.

We also now recognize those three years as being one of

the most fruitful periods in our lives. Several friends we made during that time saw the reality of Christ in the midst of our struggles. They were motivated to embark on this same journey of knowing and following him. Today, their families and friends are reaping the benefits of their faith.

Trading Weakness for Strength

LET US SUPPOSE the boss is bringing a couple of customers in from out of town this weekend to talk about our doing a product for them. He gives me the responsibility to get their business. I've never done this part of the business before and I'm scared stiff, but I want to practice this lesson of dependence. In my weakness I am to rely on God. So I'm going to use this as an opportunity to see him work.

The guests arrive. I entertain them, talk about the product—and I look to God. I ask him to give me the wisdom and the words I need. And, you know what? It's a success. The customers love the company and buy the product. The boss is happy. Everybody tells me how great I did. And I believe it. I've surprised myself. I'm even better than I thought I was! Now I'm on my way to new heights in my career.

It happens all the time. God does the work—and we take the credit. And every time we do, we mar the picture. We touch his glory.

God's strength in our weakness is a difficult truth to keep in focus. We think we've got it straight, and then we forget and we're off into our self-sufficiency again. God gave Paul a constant reminder to make sure he didn't do that. He writes, "To keep me from becoming conceited because of these surpassingly great revelations, there was given me a thorn in my flesh, a messenger of Satan, to torment me."[12]

Paul suffered from a physical disability that nagged him repeatedly. At first it didn't make sense to him. Here he was, investing all of his energy to see the gospel move forward, and then this illness hit him. He imagined how much more he could do if he just had his health back. He thought of a simple solution: He would pray to be healed. He was used to doing that for other people and had seen it happen many times. So he prayed for himself. But nothing happened. He tried it again. Still there was nothing. Then on the third try, Christ spoke. He said, Paul, you're better the way you are— weak. This way you aren't even tempted to trust in your own abilities. And everyone you go to will also know a person like you couldn't do the things you're doing. I get more glory when you have to fumble around the way you do, "for my power is made perfect in weakness."[13]

Paul's response reveals the depth of his intimacy with God. There was no questioning, no complaining or self-pity. He simply said, "Therefore I will boast all the more gladly about my weaknesses, so that Christ's power may rest on me. That is why, for Christ's sake, I delight in weaknesses, in insults, in hardships, in persecutions, in difficulties. For when I am weak, then I am strong."[14]

ONLY JARS OF CLAY WILL SERVE

We have this treasure in jars of clay to show that this all-surpassing power is from God and not from us.[15]

THAT IS WHY the jar is best made of clay. Jars of clay do a better job of revealing the treasure they contain than do jars made of finer material. Clay jars are common. They don't distract attention from the contents. There is no confusion about the source of the power. We reveal the reality of the transforming power of the gospel best when we are authentic, honest, and open about our weaknesses.

A friend from Becky's college days came to visit. She was dismissive of the gospel Becky and her husband, Don, had shared in the course of her visit. Then, on the evening before she left, Don and Becky were in tension with each other over something that had happened between the two of them. They were discouraged after they said good-bye to her. They felt they had blown it. Their words seemed to have had no effect and then they had topped off the visit with a petty disagreement between themselves.

Much to their surprise, the friend phoned a week later to tell them she had become a Christian. She explained that it was the way they had handled the disagreement that had captured her attention. She had seen how both of them had felt pain rather than going to war over their difference. *What kind of a relationship is this?* she asked herself. *What makes it work?* "Then," she said, "I realized the connection between the things you were telling me and the way you live your lives."

They had revealed Christ to her through their weakness. She could identify with that! She knew *she* was made of clay. It gave her hope to discover Don and Becky were made of the same stuff.

The truth is, we are all weak. None of us has to work at being a jar of clay because that's what we are. We all struggle with multiple inadequacies. But that is no reason to consider oneself disqualified from engaging as an insider with others. We are tempted to think we need to wait just a bit longer, until we have cleaned up a few more things, until we feel a little more competent before we actually do anything. The truth is, that day will never come. The enemy will never let us get that far away from our feelings of guilt. Further progress in our spiritual life will be minimal until we step into the light in this way. We need to engage with others, just as we are, with all our weaknesses. When we do, we will find we are on a new road to freedom, one that leads us away from the power our weaknesses have held over us. We need to live as an insider for the sake of our own spiritual progress!

LIFE PATTERNS OF A FRUITFUL INSIDER

INTRODUCTION

* * *

Life is a window of opportunity in an eternal existence. God is creating a people. He is gathering them from every corner of every nation to share eternally in his kingdom as members of his household. He has called us to partner with him in this work and has already positioned us to do this. We are an insider to various relationships within which God intends that we glorify, or reveal, him.

This call from God to participate with him is both exhilarating and intimidating! This is a purpose bigger than life. It sweeps into eternity. But we hesitate. We see the obstacles. This is going to take us beyond our comfort zones, away from the familiar faces of our little circle of people who think like we do. It will lead us into relationships with people who live differently. *Is that really okay?* we worry. *Are we really ready for this?*

Once beyond obstacles such as these we quickly face another. We don't know what to do next. Our next question is, How do we do this? In practical terms, how do we translate this vision of living as an insider into life patterns? Our purpose, in this third section, is to address this question. We will find that the Scriptures provide a surprising amount of practical guidance in how to live fruitfully as an insider. We will see that fruitful insiders live in a certain way—and consistently do certain things.

In this section we will examine seven patterns of behavior that will be part of an insider's lifestyle. Our prayer is that after reading each one, you will say to yourself, *That's really simple! I can do that.* These patterns *are* simple. But, taken together, they are powerful. That is because you will be partnering with God himself and with your sisters and brothers in Christ.

The seven life patterns are (1) taking little initiatives, (2) praying and responding, (3) serving and being served, (4) teaming up, (5) conversing the faith, (6) letting the Scriptures speak, and (7) midwifing conversion.

CHAPTER 11

THE FIRST LIFE PATTERN
OF AN INSIDER:
TAKING LITTLE INITIATIVES

People in Jesus' day did not comprehend what he had to say about the kingdom of God. Here he was, the King himself, bringing his kingdom right into their midst, and people disregarded its arrival. It wasn't what they were looking for. This kingdom had no material wealth to display, no armies to impose its power, no visible means of enforcing its rule. They did not comprehend the nature of this kingdom. People did not see that, although apparently insignificant, it is incomparably more valuable than everything else combined. Those who understand the kingdom and its ways see through this preference for the grandiose. They see through our hunt for a "silver bullet" — something spectacular and expensive that will win the world for Jesus in the next few years. They know the kingdom of God advances in people's hearts as its citizens go through their daily lives living according to Christ's rule. They understand the eternal importance little initiatives can have in this. Such initiatives are a part of their life pattern.

* * *

I n one of his metaphors, Jesus described the children of the kingdom of God as being like seeds sown in the world. With this
he is telling us that our place for now—as citizens of the kingdom—is in the world, right among the weeds. That is where we belong
because, as Jesus said, "The kingdom of God is within you."[1] If people
are going to see the kingdom of God today, they will have to observe it
in its citizens. It is revealed as Christ's rule in our heart is expressed in
our actions. People see the kingdom whenever we show mercy instead
of judgment, speak truth when a lie would be to our advantage, or serve
when it's neither expected nor deserved.

IT'S YOUR MOVE!

THIS IDEA THAT the kingdom advances in the course of everyday life for
its citizens is implicit in several of the metaphors Jesus used to describe it.
It is like yeast, salt, seeds, or the light of a candle. Yeast permeates. So does
salt. Seeds germinate and light shines—*all without even making a sound*!
In practice, this means kingdom citizens are just different from the rest.
When they realize they have offended someone, they drop whatever they're
doing—even if it's worshiping God—and go reconcile with that person.
They keep their anger in check. They don't degrade another person by lust-
ing for them. They keep their word and are generous even toward people
who want to take advantage of them. They even love their enemies.[2]

Notice that all of these characteristics of kingdom behavior have one
thing in common. No one else can do any of them for another person! One
can't hire any of them done no matter how much money he might have.
Every kingdom citizen is called upon to take these little initiatives every day.

The problem is, many of these initiatives are so contrary to our normal responses we conclude Jesus somehow didn't really mean what he
said. Take, for example, loving one's enemy. Because it doesn't make sense

to us we tend to discount it. But Jesus meant what he said. He pointed to his Father as the model for what he was talking about. He said,

> "You have heard that it was said, 'Love your neighbor and hate your enemy.' But I tell you: Love your enemies and pray for those who persecute you, that you may be sons of your Father in heaven. He causes his sun to rise on the evil and the good, and sends rain on the righteous and the unrighteous. If you love those who love you, what reward will you get? Are not even tax collectors doing that? And if you greet only your brothers, what are you doing more than others? Do not even pagans do that? Be perfect, therefore, as your heavenly Father is perfect."[3]

Recently I was in an African country meeting with a little group of people who are engaged in communicating the gospel in their society. My roommate for the week, Chinua, had lost his brother-in-law and his nephew three weeks earlier when some Muslims attacked their home. They burned the house, and then when the father and son fled they caught them and killed them with their machetes. Several times in that week I would come into our room and find Chinua prostrate on the floor in prayer, dealing with his grief.

One morning, as we began our session, Chinua asked to say something. The day before, we had discussed this passage from Matthew, and Chinua had a comment to make. He said, "I find these verses about loving and greeting one's enemy to be especially challenging. What am I to do when the first person I meet on the road in the morning is the one who killed my brother and nephew the day before? Does God really intend that I greet that person?"

Then he went on to say, "Yes, I believe that's what he means. But this is very hard for me."

When we hear stories like Chinua's, we begin to see how radical Jesus' call to live as kingdom citizens really is. It's a lifestyle consisting of small but often very significant things, in that they are contrary to the ways of our society and our religious culture.

God loves people whether they love him back or not. The farmer who hates God gets just as much sun and rain on his crops as does his neighbor the next farm over, who loves God. Why do the wicked prosper? They prosper because God loves them! Jesus is saying, You do the same. Love the people in your life without having an agenda for them. Love them because God loves them.

Frequently someone will ask Mike or me the question, How long should I stick with a friendship? I've been a friend to this person for almost two years and he's no closer to becoming a Christian now than he was when we first met. Should I forget him and move on? The reply, of course, is, If that is our agenda in our friendships, if we are interested in people only because of what we might accomplish with them, then we have missed the point. When we think like that, we aren't loving as our heavenly Father does. He loves with no strings attached.

THE POWER IN A GREETING

THIS IDEA OF taking little initiatives in expressing love for people is so foundational, Jesus wanted to be sure we got it right. He told us exactly how to go about it. He said, "If you greet only your brothers, what are you doing more than others?" In other words, say "hello" to people! He is saying, greet the people in your daily traffic pattern that you customarily ignore. You know how that works. For most of us, our lives run on a schedule. We have to be up at a certain time because we have to be on the road at a certain time if we are to catch the train that will get us into the office by eight o'clock. The rest of the day is equally predictable.

In the course of our day we cross paths with many of the same people, day after day. (Most people live their lives on similar, predictable schedules.)

Some of these we pause and greet. We ask them how their weekends went. We wish them a happy birthday. Some we greet by name, and others with just a smile or a nod. The rest we ignore. We pass them as if they were pieces of furniture or the copy machine. And they do the same with us.

Those are the ones, Jesus is saying. Those are the people—the ones you habitually ignore—they are the ones I especially want you to greet! When you do that, you are obeying me!

Apparently, the categories that divide society haven't changed all that much between Jesus' time and ours. We've changed the labels, but the same social groupings are still with us. Jesus was addressing people who saw themselves as part of the dominant religious culture. They had erected walls between themselves and the rest of society and were living their entire lives within their little enclaves. They had the support of their theology to justify their position. Jesus is saying, Break out of that! Surprise someone today. Say hello to someone you've been ignoring. Keep at it. One day they'll make eye contact with you in response. Then they'll smile, and the next thing you know they'll be greeting you back. Do that for me!

Monday through Friday, Marcie would rise early, drive to the train station, and board the train for the forty-five-minute commute to Boston. There she would transfer to the subway that took her to her office. She made that same daily commute for a year. Then she resigned from her job to train as a physician's assistant. The subway engineer gave her a free two-week pass for her last weeks of commuting! On the last day of her customary commute, the passengers on the train threw a farewell party for her.

How do you suppose that happened? What would motivate a bunch of commuters to throw a party for another passenger? Normally, commuters will either anesthetize themselves with their newspapers, paperbacks, and Walkmans, or they will escape into their virtual offices by booting up their laptops as soon as they are seated on the train. What's the story?

Marcie is twenty-two years old. In her own words, she's "not a real extrovert." But as a follower of Christ, she decided she would apply his instructions as we've been talking about them in this chapter. She chose to ride in the same train car every day. Because that's what most people do, she was riding daily with the same people. She also *chose to be present* among the other passengers. She began to greet them. She learned people's names and got to know about their families, concerns, and interests. Some conversations would continue from one train ride to another. People got the message. Marcie was actually interested in them! Because her faith is a natural part of who she is, that too was a part of her conversations. The spontaneous party on that commuter train demonstrates the kind of response Marcie's little initiatives received.

What's in a Name?

EVERYONE CAN GREET another person. One needn't be an extrovert to do that. We greet people as an act of worship to Christ.[4] As in Marcie's story, one thing will lead to another, unforced. One day we will find ourselves standing next to someone we've exchanged greetings with, and we introduce ourselves. We exchange names. When you do that, don't lose that name. It opens the door to the rest.

I'm bad with names, you say. Most people are. So write the name down. Then you'll be good with names! From then on use the person's name in your greeting. The other person probably won't remember yours, but as you use hers, she will be motivated to learn yours. Names are important. Decades ago Dale Carnegie understood the importance of using names in the course of one's business. He said, "Remember that a man's name is the sweetest and most important sound in any language."[5] You have a person's attention when you use his or her name.

Where does this take us? It takes us as far as we need to go for now. We are ready to talk about the second life pattern of the insider.

CHAPTER 12

THE SECOND LIFE PATTERN OF AN INSIDER: PRAYING AND RESPONDING

* * *

The most important use of any person's name is when we repeat it in God's presence.

Several years ago our family moved into a new neighborhood as it was being built up. A new neighborhood offers certain advantages. Because everyone is new to the area and relational lines have not yet been formed, people are especially open to connecting with their neighbors. Soon after we settled in, Marge and I, together with another neighbor, took a little initiative. We wanted to stimulate a sense of community by helping people meet one another. So we organized a neighborhood crime-watch.

Our local police department promotes the organizing of neighborhood crime-watch groups. They provide the orientation and materials for any neighborhood that is interested. We contacted the police department, and one evening a policeman came to our home, where all of our neighbors had gathered for the occasion.

The policeman instructed us to make everyone's name and phone number available to each other in case of emergency. A piece of paper was passed around and we wrote our names and addresses on it. One neighbor took the names. She drew a map of the neighborhood showing all the houses and streets and the names of everyone living in all the houses. She then mailed a copy of the map to every household.

When our copy arrived in the mail, I realized I had just received my prayer list! I began to use the map in my times alone with God. I would put my finger on a house and pray for the names of the people living in it. Sometimes, because of my frightfully limited attention span when I pray, I would walk through the neighborhood, praying for people as I passed their houses. I found that helped me stay focused.

It's easy to remember people's names when you are praying for them, so it didn't take long for me to know the names of everyone in the neighborhood. When I'd see my neighbor across the cul-de-sac getting into his car I'd shout a greeting to him: "Hello, Dan!"

Surprised at hearing his name, he would look up and shout, "Hi there, how are ya!"

After a few such exchanges he apparently got out his copy of that map. He was ready for me the next time. When I greeted him, he shouted back, "Hi, Jim!"

Friendship was imminent from that point on. He had made the effort to learn my name. We both felt good about that.

JOIN GOD IN WHAT HE'S DOING

OCCASIONALLY I WILL meet a person who has determined to evangelize his entire neighborhood. One couple distributed books to all their neighbors. Later they sent out invitations to everyone, inviting them to attend an evangelistic event in their home. Sometimes such efforts bear fruit—but they often backfire. An initiative of this sort is too impersonal to be well received in a neighbor-to-neighbor situation. By trying to move too far too fast, rapport is lost. And the initiators find themselves left out of things from then on.

Marge and I don't have the capacity to relate to all our neighbors. We have neither the time nor the energy. But we can do something with a few. Who should those few be? That's another place where prayer comes in.

We can assume God is at work, drawing some of the people whose names are on our Neighborhood Watch map to himself. We can also assume that as we pray he will guide us to those people. The apostle Paul, as we saw in the previous chapter, talked about having certain people written on his heart by the Holy Spirit. The fact that certain people were there, in his heart, gave him the guidance he needed to know what God wanted him to do. I find God will do the same with us.

As I prayed over the map of our neighborhood, a pattern developed. I would move quickly over some of the names. Then, I would linger more over some of the others. I would stop and pray in more detail for a few. Whenever I would cross paths with someone among those few, I was especially aware. God was guiding me to join him in his work among my neighbors.

This illustration I have used of our neighborhood should not confine our thinking. Jesus' use of the word *neighbor* is broader than mine here. In answer to the question, "Who is my neighbor?" Jesus told a story about a Samaritan who came across someone who was beaten up and needing help. The Samaritan was the "good neighbor" even though he had never before laid eyes on him. Neighborliness has nothing to do with where one's house is located. Your "neighbors" may be in your workplace, your dorm, among your professional associates, or on your sports team.

It helps to listen to God before we act. Newly wed, our daughter Michelle and her husband, Glenn, set out to offer Christ to some of their friends. They spent their next three years dropping good seed onto some very hard soil. What happened to the seed? "The birds came and ate it up."[1] Seeing no spiritual progress among their friends, they began to wonder if God would ever use them for anything. Then they moved to another state where Glenn did his postgraduate studies. This time they prayed their way forward, and God led them into fruitfulness.

PRAY A STEP AT A TIME

JESUS FREQUENTLY USED agricultural metaphors to describe the way people enter the kingdom. With these metaphors he communicated the idea that conversion doesn't just suddenly happen out of nothing. When it takes place it is because seed has been sown, watered, and cultivated. It has had time to germinate. Finally, harvest time comes. Understanding this truth—that evangelism is a process rather than an event—is fundamental to our fruitfulness as an insider.

Sowing and reaping are different activities with different goals. Often our popular notion of evangelism includes little more than reaping. For many, evangelism consists of leading people into making a decision. All their efforts are oriented around that event. This notion puts all but very few beyond the reach of our witness. But when we understand that the gospel needs to grow in a person's heart before it can bear fruit, our opportunities widen significantly. Suddenly we find we have access to many. And we gain patience, the kind a farmer has as he waits for his harvest to ripen.

We tend our field through prayer. Are there rocks in the soil of a heart? What are they? Is the soil hard? Why? What can be planted now? What about the weeds that threaten to choke the growth? How do I cultivate what's growing?

As we pray, God will guide us. Prayer isn't just talking to God. It's interacting with him. It involves listening. It includes being predisposed to respond to what God puts in our heart. Prayer often leads to action. It is not a sedentary activity at all. Jesus said that "everyone who asks and keeps on asking receives; and he who seeks and keeps on seeking finds; and to him who knocks and keeps on knocking, the door shall be opened."[2]

There are times as I'm praying for someone that I know exactly what I'm supposed to do next. But the idea frightens me. It calls for more boldness than I am comfortable with. The temptation is to shut down and stay where I am—maybe pray a little bit more.

What I need to do at those times is get up, ask for boldness and for the words to go with it, and go do what I'm told. I've done that many times, often with my knees knocking, only to discover God had been there at work, answering my prayers, preparing the way for my doing what he was prompting me to do.

What Does God Do in Response to Our Prayers?

PRAYER IS A request for the Holy Spirit's active participation in a situation. It brings divine resources to bear on what's going on. As Jesus explained the coming of the Holy Spirit to his disciples, he said, "When he comes, he will convict the world of guilt in regard to sin and righteousness and judgment." Isn't that exactly what needs to happen in the hearts of our unbelieving friends? How are they to have any concern for their true spiritual condition if they don't realize how things are, in reality, between themselves and God?

Jesus went on to explain: He, the Holy Spirit, will convict:

- "in regard to sin, because men do not believe in me." (Believing in Christ is the linchpin of our relationship with God. Unbelief is the sin that keeps someone under God's judgment.)

- "in regard to righteousness, because I am going to the Father, where you can see me no longer." (As long as Jesus walked the earth he served as the measuring stick for righteousness. His life was a walking definition of the term. Now that Jesus is not physically present, the Holy Spirit does this work.)

- "and in regard to judgment, because the prince of this world now stands condemned."[3] (This world is doomed. Its leader, Satan, and all who are with him are being destroyed. So don't gamble your life on something that has no future!)

This is Jesus' sobering summary of the unbeliever's status. It also describes what we can expect the Holy Spirit to do in the hearts of those we pray for. We can ask God to act on these matters with the confidence that we are praying his will.

It is also very important to remember the *division of labor* in this work of bringing people into a relationship with Christ. I can't convict anyone of sin, nor can I show someone what true righteousness looks like. I can't make another person realize he is building his life on something that is already doomed. I find, in fact, that when I do get into such subjects, the conversation wears thin very quickly. I begin to sound moralistic. It is better to talk to God about them and ask for the Holy Spirit to do the convincing.

Alceu was a second-year medical student at the Universidade de Parana in Brazil. Over a period of several months we read and discussed our way through several chapters of the gospel of John. Although professing atheism, he was intrigued by the intellectual challenge of Jesus' teachings. But I was becoming concerned about our progress because our discussions were all so cerebral. Repeatedly, I tried to move things from the world of ideas toward matters of the heart, but without success. So I decided to pray that God would take away Alceu's ability to sleep or study until he put his faith in Christ.

After praying this way for a couple weeks, Alceu and I met again. As we greeted each other I asked him how he was doing. He replied, "I don't know what's wrong with me. Lately I haven't been able to sleep or study." We can create the opportunity for a person to get a good look at Christ, but we can't touch the heart. That's for God to do.

PERSEVERE!

IT DOESN'T ALWAYS happen that we get to follow through on our prayers, as I was able to with Alceu. Many times there is no opportunity for the person who is doing the praying to even see the results of his or her prayers.

Through her job of caring for terminally ill people, Audrey met a woman we'll call Mary. Mary was dying of cancer. Although she had been very involved for over five years in a community arts and crafts group run by a local church, Mary herself did not have a faith.

On discovering that Audrey had a faith, Mary asked if she would mind answering some questions about spiritual issues. Over time it became obvious to Audrey that Mary had put her faith in Jesus Christ. In the months that followed, Mary continued to look to her for encouragement.

Mary had the support of many friends in her illness. Along with her family, many of her friends from the arts and crafts group would visit her. She was also supported by a couple she and her husband had been friends with since they were in their twenties. But they now lived on the other side of the world. In the last weeks of her life Mary talked daily on the phone with that couple.

All of Mary's friends from the arts and crafts group attended her funeral. The couple that had been friends with her for so many years also made the trip. They spoke at the funeral. The husband began by saying they had been best friends with Mary and her husband for thirty years.

Then, to Audrey's surprise, he went on to tell the audience they had prayed regularly over those years that Mary would "come to know and love our friend, Jesus." He described their joy as they saw those prayers answered in the last six months of her life.

Audrey also discovered that Mary's friends from the arts and crafts group had been praying for her. Their prayer was that Mary would find comfort and hope in Jesus Christ. God had used various people from various situations and places to draw this woman to himself. Some planted, others cultivated, and Audrey had the joy of reaping!

Distance is not a factor in God's ability to work in a life. It really makes no difference to him if we are sitting beside the person we are praying for or are on the other side of the world. Proximity may help us with our faith in our asking, but it makes no difference to God in his answering!

CONCLUSION

Devote yourselves to prayer, being watchful and thankful.[4] As we pray we need to keep our eyes open to what God is doing in response to our prayers. We thank him, even as we ask because we trust him with the outcome.

WE HAVE LOOKED at two of the most foundational life patterns for an insider: *taking little initiatives* and *praying*. Both are simple in that neither requires unusual gifting or ability, but both are powerful. If we take nothing more from this book than these two ideas and begin to practice them, God will use us in ways we never imagined.

CHAPTER 13

THE THIRD LIFE PATTERN OF AN INSIDER: SERVING OTHERS

On June 4, 1989, the image of a lone protester stand-ing face to face with an army tank in Tiananmen Square in Beijing, China, grabbed the attention of the entire world. The picture said it all. The heavy hand of China's Communist regime was being chal-lenged by its people.

✳ ✳ ✳

Last year, twelve years after that event, Mike and I were in Asia for a meeting with a group of people from across the continent. They had gathered to learn what they could from one another on how to effectively spread the gospel within their countries. Kim, one of the protesters who had been in Tiananmen Square, was present. For him, Tiananmen Square marked the beginning of a spiritual quest that led him to Christ. It began with a simple act of service by an elderly woman.

On May 29, 1989, Kim and a friend were in the square to protest the

Communist regime. They had sliced their hands and drawn blood to write their message on white headbands, which they were wearing. Kim had written the word *Freedom* on his. His friend had written *Democracy* on his. They were harassing the soldiers and helping block the army vehicles from entering the square. It was summertime and very hot. After twenty-four hours of duty, the soldiers were hungry and thirsty. They had had nothing to eat or drink. Then Kim saw an elderly woman, a professor from the university, making the rounds of the soldiers, serving them bread and water! He was stunned.

"Later," Kim told us, "I asked her why she did that." She replied, "The soldiers did not know what they were doing—and I was there to protect the students."

"This was my first direct experience with Christianity," Kim said. "She was the first Christian I had ever met. Until then I had thought Christianity to be ridiculous, a religion of foreigners. But now I thought, *This is a good, kind religion. The Christian God must be a kind God.*

Three years later Kim was studying for his master's degree at another university. There he met a Christian who invited him to study John's gospel together with some other students. He was impressed with the others in the circle of friends and with the Jesus he saw in the Scriptures. His first impression was, *Jesus is kind, and he's smart!*

Now Kim is good seed in the soil of China. The elderly professor has no idea what her act of service set into motion. Indeed, she wasn't even thinking about the possible effects of her actions. For her, it was simply a matter of obeying the Great Commandment to "love your neighbor as yourself."[1]

The Great Commandment

A LAWYER HAD listened to Jesus long enough to realize that what he was saying didn't fit with the orthodox theology of the day. Jesus' teachings were filled with talk about eternal life and how to have it. *Very strange,* the lawyer thought. *Maybe I can catch him in a violation of our law, and we'll have something to charge him with.* So he asked, "What must I do to inherit eternal life?"

Jesus replied, You're a lawyer; how do you read the law on it?

The lawyer, quoting from the book of Leviticus, replied, "'Love the Lord your God with all your heart and with all your soul and with all your strength and with all your mind'; and, 'Love your neighbor as yourself.'"

Jesus replied, "You have answered correctly. . . . Do this and you will live."

With this, Jesus turned the whole discussion upside down. Suddenly the lawyer found himself on the defensive! He found some of his neighbors disgusting. They were ignorant and dirty—unlovable. "Neighbor" certainly couldn't mean them. So he asked, "Who is my neighbor?"

Jesus answered this question with a little story about a traveler who was beaten up, stripped and robbed, and then left alongside a road, half-dead. A priest hurried past without stopping. So did a Levite. Finally a Samaritan—the same kind of trash the lawyer found intolerable in his neighborhood—stopped and helped.

Then Jesus asked, because we're defining *neighbor*, "Which of these three do you think was a neighbor to the man?"

The lawyer could only reply that it was "the one who had mercy on him."

With that reply, Jesus had him. He said, "Go and do likewise."[2] Imagine what went through that lawyer's mind from then on, every time he found himself around the neighbors he disliked so much! Jesus awakened him to his own failure to keep the law.

On another occasion, Jesus identified those same two commandments as being the synthesis of the entire biblical message. He said, "'Love the Lord your God with all your heart and with all your soul and with all your mind.' This is the first and greatest commandment. And the second is like it: 'Love your neighbor as yourself.' All the Law and the prophets hang on these two commandments."[3]

That is an astonishing thing to say. With it, Jesus reduced the message of the entire Old Testament down to two sentences. If anything deserves our attention, those two sentences do!

What does it mean, in practice, to love God and our neighbor? *Love* is a verb. It calls for action. If we obeyed these two commandments, we would be expressing our love for God by serving our neighbors. That is the very essence of insidership. If we lived by them, our message to the world would be irresistible!

But many of us have the same problem the lawyer did. When we read, "Love your neighbor as yourself," we think, *That, of course, refers to my Christian neighbors.* Are we not to give special attention to serving one another within the body? Besides, we argue, believers don't have enough in common with unbelievers to really be friends with them.

This kind of thinking denies the Great Commandment and deprives the church of the power it needs to fulfill its calling to go to the world.

THE POWER OF SERVING

FOR YEARS THIS story of the "Good Samaritan" bothered me. It seemed so, well, *wimpish.* Is Jesus saying that the bottom line, really, is just to show mercy? Is that all we are to do? Something, I thought, has to be missing from the story. Certainly Jesus meant we should at least include a clear presentation of the gospel in the course of our helping someone. But he didn't say that. The point of his little story is simple. We fulfill the law of love by serving the needs of the people with whom we cross paths.

Once again Jesus is keeping things simple for our sake. There are countless ways to serve. Anyone can do it. It doesn't take special talent or gifting. We serve our neighbor when we pick up her mail and water her plants while she's away on a trip. We serve when we welcome a new arrival into the neighborhood with a plant and our phone number to call when they have questions. We serve our neighbor at work when we do a little extra to help him meet his deadline on a project. Serving is another of those simple ideas that is foundational to fruitful insidership. Simply put, it is meeting another person's need because we are motivated by a desire to express love and gratitude to Christ for his unspeakable service to us. This kind of service speaks volumes without our saying a word. Christ will be seen.

A few years ago, Paula, a neighbor, sprained her ankle so badly she was immobilized, unable to step on one foot at all. They had two growing children, and her husband, Jerry, was at a complete loss in the kitchen.

The following afternoon I walked into our kitchen and found Marge busy cooking. A cardboard box was on the kitchen counter. I asked her what she was doing. She said, "I'm feeding the Swensons." She had prepared a meal and was about to carry it over to their house. She continued to do this daily until Paula was able to take over again. Later, when we invited several of our neighbors to join us to explore the Bible together, their participation wasn't ever in question. They had been waiting for us to get going.

LET OTHERS SERVE YOU

JESUS SAID, "IT is more blessed to give than to receive."[4] It is also *easier* for most of us! Many people have difficulty receiving anything from anyone. But where there is giving, there has to be receiving. Not wanting to receive can be a subtle form of pride that deprives the other of something they need to do. Jesus knew how to receive.

Mary had a wild idea. She had gone out and bought a bottle of perfume that had cost her a fortune—a year's salary! When the moment was right she was going to pour it on Jesus. She wasn't just going to give it to him to take home and use a dab at a time on special occasions. At the appropriate time, she was going to empty the whole bottle on him.

Mary, her sister Martha, and their brother Lazarus had planned a dinner in honor of Jesus. The occasion was even more extraordinary than her extravagant plan. A few weeks earlier, Jesus had come to their home in Bethany and had raised Lazarus from the dead! *What can we do,* they must have wondered, *to express our gratitude?*

At the dinner, while they were reclining at the table, Mary took out the perfume, poured it out on Jesus' feet, and wiped his feet with her hair. Judas, knowing what that bottle had cost, and seeing it used up so wantonly, objected. What a waste![5]

What if Jesus had felt the same way Judas did about Mary's action? Jesus didn't *need* that perfume poured onto him. What if he had said, No, Mary, don't do that. That's too extravagant. Take your perfume, sell it, and do something more responsible with the money.

Mary would have done that if Jesus had told her to. And she would have felt awkward and stupid for even thinking of doing what she had intended. Her excitement would have been dashed, her thankfulness left unexpressed. Jesus served Mary by letting her serve him. She grew in her love for him that day.

A part of loving our neighbors is letting them serve us. Serving needs to be mutual if it is to be healthy. We can create the opportunity for that. We can borrow our neighbors' skills when we need them; or get them to help when we need one more strong back or let them loan us some salt because we've run out. Friendships are forged in the mutuality of giving and receiving.

HOSPITALITY

HAVE YOU EVER noticed how much of Jesus' life revolved around eating? One of his first public appearances was at a wedding, where he contributed to the feast by providing the wine. A little later he was at Matthew's house for a dinner party with Matthew's old friends. Then, on another occasion, he invited himself over for dinner at Zacchaeus's house. His parables are filled with stories of banquets and feasts. Just about the last thing he did before he was arrested and killed was to have a meal with the Twelve. Then after he rose from the dead he met them again on the beach, where he served them some baked fish.

And it's not over. He said that when we see him again, "he will dress himself to serve, will have them recline at the table and will come and wait on them."[6] He will hold a banquet for his servants—and will wait on the tables himself! Can you imagine that!

What is this thing about eating? Obviously there is more to it than just fueling the body. In the culture of the first century, eating with someone was a statement of mutuality. It was an expression of *koinonia*, of having a common bond with the other. That was why people were so incensed that Jesus ate with Matthew's friends. Devout people of the day wouldn't think of doing that. They asked Jesus, "Why do you eat and drink with tax collectors and 'sinners'?"

Jesus replied, "I have not come to call the righteous, but sinners to repentance."[7] Apparently he needed to eat with unbelievers to accomplish this purpose. So do we.

On one occasion Jesus was having dinner at a Pharisee's house. It was on the Sabbath. At one point in the course of the meal, Jesus turned to his host and said, "When you give a luncheon or dinner, do not invite your friends, your brothers or relatives, or your rich neighbors; if you do, they may invite you back and so you will be repaid." That's how life works. We have our family, our circle of friends—and we spend our life inviting each other back and forth. In the end we break even. It hasn't cost us a thing.

"But," Jesus continued, "when you give a banquet, invite the poor, the crippled, the lame, the blind, and you will be blessed."[8] In other words, invite those outside your ordinary circle of friends; those same people you usually don't greet when you meet them on the street; those who have been crippled from being under Satan's dominion, crashing around in the dark all their lives.

WHAT'S IN A MEAL?

WHY DO WE have to eat with these people? What's in a meal? As Americans, we have probably forgotten the answer to this. We seldom dine. Instead, we refuel—in mid-air!

I recently watched a news clip on the problem of obesity in the United States. Why, the researchers wondered, are Americans so fat while the French—known for their love of food—are so thin? The video showed a French housewife at the market, making her purchases in preparation for a meal. She carefully chose a vegetable, poked the eye of the fish she purchased, and selected some pieces of fruit.

The next scene showed a French chef preparing a meal and arranging it onto the plates. Dessert was a few small cubes of something obviously sweet and tasty, with a bit of sauce dribbled over it. The whole presentation was a work of art.

Then the camera panned to a McDonald's counter in the United States where a customer was carrying a tray piled high with a multilayered hamburger and French fries, and a pail-sized container of Coke tucked in alongside. The French chef came back on and expressed his wonderment at American eating habits. "Once," he said, "I saw someone eating a piece of pizza while driving a car! I hear some even watch television while they eat! They get distracted and forget they're eating. In contrast," he said, "the French do nothing else while they dine. The meal is the event."

Hospitality, someone said, is the blend of attention and space. Serving a meal is an expression of hospitality. It does not have to be a gourmet meal. The food can be most simple. A sandwich will do, but when food is accompanied by an atmosphere of unhurried acceptance, it becomes a feast.

Have you ever noticed how conversation over a meal in a quiet place is different from conversation anywhere else? People mostly talk about other people. Events and stories of events are also common topics of discussion. Both of those topics leave us on the surface of things. When we move into conversation about ideas, we have begun to go beneath the surface; and when we begin to talk about how we *feel* about those ideas, we have begun to really understand one another. But this takes time.

I have seen many Christians get this far into a great evening—and then blow it. It is because they feel it will all be a waste if they don't get in, at least, a little commercial for Jesus! It is better to relax and enjoy your guests, with no other agenda. The words can come later, as ultimately all topics lead to Jesus.

CONCLUSION

HOSPITALITY IS LISTED as one of the qualifications for an elder.[9] It's there for a good reason. The church is about people—and where people are involved, hospitality must follow. We certainly will not be fruitful as an insider if we are unwilling to offer hospitality.

There needs to be small talk, the kind that happens around a meal—about people and things—before deeper things can be discussed with any freedom. I find it difficult to invite an unbeliever to read the Bible with me before we've eaten together.

Jesus finished his suggestion to his host with the observation, "When you give a banquet, invite the poor, the crippled, the lame, the blind, and you will be blessed. Although they cannot repay you, you will be repaid at the resurrection of the righteous."[10] I want to be there watching when that elderly Chinese woman steps into God's presence and discovers what God has done to multiply the effects of her simple act of giving a little bread and water to some soldiers!

CHAPTER 14

THE FOURTH LIFE PATTERN OF AN INSIDER: CONVERSING THE FAITH

* * *

Mike began to follow Christ while he was completing his final year of teacher training. This new faith brought profound changes into his life—and a desire to let others know about Christ. In the course of his spiritual growth, Mike sought out help from several more mature Christians in how to share his faith.

Mike soon discovered there was more to talking to others about Christ than he had imagined. He was taught to tell in just three minutes his story of how he came to faith. He wrote it out and committed it to memory. He also learned to clearly present the gospel in a coherent, concise way. And he learned how to approach strangers, engage them in conversation, and find out if they would be interested in hearing more of what he had to say.

Equipped with these new skills, Mike began to visit the Botanical Gardens on Sunday afternoons. He went there to share his faith. As he strolled into the gardens, he would pray for boldness and keep his eye open for opportunities to converse with people. Occasionally he was successful, but most people politely refused to engage in conversation with him. Some resented his intrusion into their leisure time. This didn't bother Mike too much. He was, he reasoned, just suffering a bit for his faith.

Monday through Friday was another story. Mike had gotten a teaching job in an elementary school where he worked side by side with the rest of the teaching staff. He wondered how to apply his newly acquired skills among his fellow teachers. The time never seemed right to interrupt conversations to make a presentation like he had been trained to do. He tried several times, but it didn't go well. This was both frustrating and discouraging. He resorted to asking some of the staff to attend some Christian meetings with him, but no one showed interest. Frustrated and at a loss about what to do next, Mike began to withdraw socially.

Mike was doing what he had been taught to do in the seminar, but it had backfired on him. What had gone wrong?

EVANGELIST OR INSIDER?

MIKE, LIKE SO many thousands of others, had been trained in an approach to evangelism that did not serve him in his daily life. Gifted missionary evangelists had taught him skills and methods they used in their own work as evangelists. And they worked, to a degree, for Mike on Sunday afternoons in the Botanical Gardens. There, people who didn't want to talk, or who took offense, could simply move on. And so could he. He could talk to the next person that happened by. But on the job, he and his fellow teachers had to work together, whether they liked it or not. Disappointed with this response in such close quarters, Mike began to compartmentalize his life into work and ministry. Ministry, he concluded, was something he would do on Sundays. What Mike really needed, but did not realize at the time, was to learn to relate to his colleagues as an insider rather than as an evangelist.

We often fail to make the distinction between what is appropriate for evangelists or apostles, who, in the course of their ministry, *proclaim* the gospel, and what is appropriate for insiders, who are to *converse* their faith. Our failure to make this distinction leaves many would-be insiders feeling like failures. After a few painful attempts within their circle of relationships, they give up on trying to share their faith. They quit, and then spend the remainder of their lives in guilty silence. Occasionally they might say something to a stranger.

The apostle Paul makes very clear the distinction between the approach the apostle takes and the ways of the insider in the concluding remarks of his letter to the believers in Colosse. "Devote yourselves to prayer," he writes. "And pray for us, too, that God may open a door for our message, so that we may proclaim the mystery of Christ, for which I am in chains."[1]

This is so typical of Paul. His primary concern was to get a hearing where he could proclaim the gospel. It didn't matter to him whether some of his listeners liked it or not, or whether or not he ended up in jail for his efforts. He was asking prayer for just two things: opportunities and the ability to take advantage of them. But notice the difference in what he encouraged the believers in Colosse to do with their witness. To them he says, "Be wise in the way you act toward outsiders; make the most of every opportunity. Let your conversation be always full of grace, seasoned with salt, so that you may know how to answer everyone."[2]

For those believers who were insiders to their society, Paul's first concern was for their manner of life, their actions. They were to respond to opportunities with actions. Then, in that context, their conversations were to be like *salty morsels*. You can't eat just one! Take one, and you're back for another until the bowl is empty. In other words, Paul is saying, converse your faith in such a manner that people will ask for more! And then be ready.

Mike did not have this distinction clear in his mind. He understood that being a witness for Christ meant presenting the gospel to another person. He saw it as a verbal exercise, accomplished when the other person had heard what he had to say. With that definition, about the only thing he knew to do was to *hijack* a conversation and make his presentation. So that's what he did.

We have all had the experience of having a conversation hijacked. There we are, in what we think is a casual, informal discussion, when all of a sudden the other person slips into a subject he or she has already rehearsed—which is obviously headed in a predetermined direction. A yellow light goes on in our head, and we wonder what the other person is selling. As Danny DiVito's character in *The Big Kahuna* put it, "When you hijack a conversation, it is no longer a conversation. It is a sales pitch. It is a sales pitch, whether you are talking about [the product] or about Jesus Christ."[3]

Mike didn't need to hijack the conversation with his workmates. They were going to see each other again tomorrow, the next day, and every other day during that semester. He should have, instead, slipped them a bite of something salty.

Provoking the Search

CURIOSITY MAKES PEOPLE want more. When it's satisfied, the search is over.

Jesus had just invited Philip to follow him. Excited, the first thing Philip did was find his friend Nathanael and tell him, "We have found the one Moses wrote about in the Law, and about whom the prophets also wrote—Jesus of Nazareth, the son of Joseph."

Nathanael was skeptical. "Nazareth!" he responded. "Can anything good come from there?"

"'Come and see,' said Philip."[4]

Philip provoked Nathanael's curiosity. He had to go see this man for himself. This little exchange illustrates the task of the insider. We are to provoke the search to know God among our friends. We don't have to be Bible scholars or trained teachers to do this. We do it best through the way we live our life and the manner in which we converse about our faith.

CONVERSATION, WITH SALT

CONVERSATION CAN BE described as an informal spoken exchange between two or more people. Some are more skilled at this than others. Some are born communicators. But it is a skill almost everyone can develop or at least improve upon.

When I think of a skilled conversationalist, Larry King, host of CNN's *Larry King Live,* comes to my mind. So when I came across his book, *How to Talk to Anyone, Anytime, Anywhere,* in an airport newsstand, I bought it. His essential message can be summarized in the following two points:

1. Be honest and open about yourself. Let people know how you feel about things.
2. Take a sincere interest in the other person. Ask questions, and then listen to what the other says. Listening, he says, is the first rule of good conversation.[5]

Let's look at these two points from the perspective of an insider.

Be honest and open about yourself.

Mike and I spend a lot of time on airplanes. That means we spend a lot of time conversing with people we've never met before. I've observed that conversations follow certain predictable patterns among travelers. Sometimes the person next to me just wants to be left alone. Sometimes, that's what I want. That's an easy one to communicate. A bit of body language and a few monosyllable responses are enough to send that message.

It is equally simple to signal one's willingness to converse. We probably all have the same questions in our mind when we meet a stranger. We want to know who the person is, where he's from, what he does for a living, what he's interested in, and so on. When someone readily volunteers that information, I know the door is open for conversation. And I know that when I do that, he gets that same signal.

I find similar signals at work in almost all conversations, even those that run on the deepest levels. If I hope to have meaningful communication with another, the door to my person needs to be open. I need to be forthcoming and honest about myself. When I am, the other person knows he or she has the same freedom. A kind of trust is established, a common ground upon which we can walk together.

As this trust grows, sharing my experiences in trying to walk with God begins to have a place our conversations. It fits because that's a part of my life. The Bible is filled with practical wisdom. It addresses relationship building, conflict resolution, how to handle stress, how to manage time and money, and on and on. A one-liner crediting the Scriptures as the source of an idea we're discussing often communicates more to my nonChristian friends than do my best propositions about God.

The more we understand how the gospel affects us in our daily affairs and relationships, and the more we learn to converse about this in *everyday language,* the easier it becomes to let people in on what it means to know God. Because the gospel envelops all of life—how we conduct ourselves with our family, in our society, and our work—every subject, when fully explored, will trace back to Jesus Christ, "in whom are hidden all the treasures of wisdom and knowledge."[6]

Boldness is not brashness. Boldness, for the insider, means having enough confidence in the gospel to use it as the frame of reference for living and interpreting everyday life. Growing in our understanding of the connections between the two and in how to talk about it is a worthy life-time pursuit. It also includes being authentic. We have a single version of our story that includes our experience with God. We need to work at expressing this story in familiar words that people can understand. This, I think, is what Paul meant when he told the Colossian Christians that they needed to "know how to answer everyone."[7]

Take a sincere interest in the other person. Ask questions . . .

> The purposes of a man's heart are deep waters, but a man of
> understanding draws them out.[8]

Questions are like keys that unlock the storehouses of the mind. Most people are unaware of how much they have to offer others, but good questions can bring it out. Larry King observes, "Everybody is an expert on something. Everybody's got at least one subject they love to talk about."[9] He goes on to explain that a good conversationalist will provide others with the opportunity to talk on that subject.

My favorite place in the entire world is our dining room table at home. That's where our conversations take place. It's the learning center of our household. We often have guests, and there is always something to learn from someone.

One recent evening, our table was crowded with several of our twin daughters' friends. One of them asked a question which each, in turn, had a chance to answer. The question had no special agenda, but it resulted in a discussion that was fun, and we learned a lot about each other. The question was, If you could live anywhere in the world, where would it be? Which country would it be? Why would you choose to live there?

Asking a question like this in a lighthearted atmosphere opens the way for much more. A good conversation can last for months because it consists of asking questions that are of interest to the other person and then builds on the discussion with subsequent questions. But at this point, we often become our own worst enemy. We sabotage our own conversations.

. . . and listen!

Most of us have picked up some bad listening habits along the way. As a result, we move through life shutting conversations down before they have a chance to develop.

We are bad listeners when we feel compelled to give advice or to fix somebody's problem; or when we derail the subject being discussed by introducing another, triggered by something someone said. Another common bad habit is to escalate conversations into debates over issues or beliefs. This leaves people feeling intimidated by the intensity of our feelings, and they shut down.

Sometimes we aren't quite present in the conversation. We might be looking at the speaker, nodding and maybe even smiling, but mentally we are off somewhere, attending to something else. Then, some of us don't listen because we are busy waiting our turn to talk. While we wait, we are mentally rehearsing what we're about to say. What is being said will not alter the pronouncement we are composing in our mind. We've worked too hard on it to change now.

We like to think we get by undetected with bad habits such as these, but we almost never do.

A good listener, in contrast, gives attention not only to what the other person is saying, but also to the body language and other signals the speaker is sending. The listener wants to understand not just the words but also the tenor of the conversation—the feelings that are being expressed. This type of person encourages the speaker by making eye contact and affirming him or her with corresponding signals. Good listeners honor people through their attentiveness.

"COME AND SEE"

IN TIME OUR nonChristian friends realize that our faith is significant to us. Based on their previous experiences with Christians, that realization might make them nervous. They could think, *Now what? Can I trust this person to accept me and not preach at me?*

We need to be clear in our own mind as to what it is we *do* want to see happen. We do have something in mind. We do want them to *want* to come and see—Jesus! But what will doing that look like? It helps to have a picture of where we want to go next in our journey with our nonChristian friends.

If they are to come to faith, most nonChristians today need an ongoing exposure to Jesus as the Scriptures reveal him. Peter writes, "For you have been born again, not of perishable seed, but of imperishable, through the living and enduring word of God."[10]

This means we need to be going to the Scriptures together. There are many ways to do this. One that has proven to be simple and fruitful for many has been to invite a few friends who have some affinity with one another to meet to explore the Bible. There will come a time when it will be appropriate to suggest something of this nature. On several occasions I have approached a few nonChristian friends with the invitation, "My wife and I are thinking about getting a few friends together to read the Bible. We find this helps us keep our lives on track, and we're not doing this with anyone right now. We're not ready to get started, but when we are we'll let you know."

People need time to digest an invitation like that, as the idea of doing such a thing has probably never crossed their minds. We need to give them time think about it. As we pray about their responses, the Holy Spirit will help them decide.[11]

CHAPTER 15

THE FIFTH LIFE PATTERN OF AN INSIDER: PARTNERING

We have taken initiatives, some of which are resulting in growing friendships. We have prayed for these new friends and have served them. As we have gotten to know each other, they have come to understand that we reference our lives by the Bible. They are watching us to see what that does to a person. We have suggested the possibility of getting a few of our mutual friends together to read the Bible but haven't yet asked them for a response. When the time is right, we'll get started.

* * *

Now we need to make sure we have some partners involved who can share the load in what is coming next. We are inviting a few people to "come and see." This could be as simple as meeting in someone's living room or apartment to explore the Bible as their schedules permit. This might be simple, but it is still more than one person can handle alone. We could justify this need for partnering with the fact that we wouldn't have the time or the energy to do this by ourselves, but there is a bigger reason than that. We need to partner because we were designed by God to do things this way.

PARTNERING IS GOD'S IDEA

MANY OF THE Scriptures we use to develop our doctrine of the church make the point that the church consists of people who are in Christ and who are interdependent with one another. In his letter to the Romans, Paul said that "in Christ we who are many form one body, and each member belongs to all the others."[1] Then to the Corinthians he wrote, "God has arranged the parts in the body, every one of them, just as he wanted them to be."[2] To the Ephesians he said, "From him the whole body, joined and held together by every supporting ligament, grows."[3] Peter, in his letter to Jewish believers scattered by persecution, wrote, "Each one should use whatever gift he has received to serve others, faithfully administering God's grace in its various forms."[4] The essential idea of these and other similar Scriptures is that we belong to one another, and God has gifted us to serve one another. We are, in fact, designed *against* being able to go it alone.

Just as in everything else he has created, God's design for his people displays his brilliance. He wants us to hold together, to live life together. But we'd rather strike out on our own. That's human nature. So what does he do? He glues us together by giving all of us the Holy Spirit—who gifts every person with one thing or another. But he never gives all his gifts to any *one* person. Thus, we all have something with which to serve, and we all have needs that will be unmet until someone serves us! In this way our weaknesses are as important to us as are our abilities; by them, we are bound to our brothers and sisters. Whatever we find ourselves doing as followers of Christ, we can be sure we need one another to make it happen.

It's strange that we seem to immediately understand our need for the body when it comes to worship, teaching, and prayer, but in this matter of sharing our faith, we usually think of it as being a solitary effort. The popular notion of an evangelist conjures images of a fearless individual who proclaims the gospel to a multitude or to an individual and then reports back to the body with accounts of his success. This is a flawed picture. We need one another if we are to fruitfully reveal Christ to our friends, just as we need effective help in every other area of our life.

We also need to understand that whatever gifts and abilities we might have are as useful for serving nonChristians as they are in serving our sisters and brothers. The popular excuse, "I don't have the gift of evangelism," doesn't exempt anyone from using the gifts he does have to serve his neighbors. Someone with the gift of mercy or hospitality, for example, will have more to offer most people who are at the beginning of their searches for Christ than will a "gifted evangelist." Our contribution, whatever it might be, fits when we think in terms of combining what we have with what others can bring to the effort.

CREATING A PARTNERSHIP

IT WOULD PROBABLY be an overstatement to call what we're envisioning here a "team." A team consists of people drawn together by common values for a common task. It is people working together for a common goal, each out of his or her strengths. Team members complement one another with their strengths and compensate for each other's weaknesses. A team gives focused attention to a task.

Insider partners follow the same principle of interdependence, but they tend to be more informal than a team. A partnership would consist of another couple, or one or two other singles. The ideal (which never seems to exist) would be to have as a partner another Christian friend who travels in the same circle of relationships we do. Because that situation doesn't happen very often, we usually need to find a creative alternative.

Several years ago a change in my responsibilities meant a move to a new city for our family. As we settled into our new house, we began to think about finding some friends who would be interested in getting together to read the Scriptures. We made this a primary subject in our prayers. We didn't know any Christians to partner with, so we set out to make a few friends among our neighbors. This was complicated by my work, which required considerable travel. Frequently I would be away for two or three weeks at a time.

These absences frustrated our efforts to get to know people well enough for them to entrust us with their friendships. Not much happened for several months. We needed a team to help maintain continuity. Then we saw it, right there in front of us. Three of our four kids had made friends with a sister and brother. Todd was playing with Orlando and the twins were playing with Anelise. We did have a team, after all. It was our own children.

Marge and I got to know the parents, Umberto and Doris. We visited some of their favorite restaurants together. Umberto and I went to soccer games. Then I would vanish on one of my trips. But the "team" kept at it. Our children kept playing together. So, when I returned home, we could pick up where we left off.

As we prayed, our next step became clear. One evening, Marge and I went over to our neighbors' house and I said something like this: "We like to get together with friends to read the Bible. It helps us keep our lives pointed in the right direction. We don't have anything like that going on right now, and, as you know, my travels make it hard for us to do anything like that with much continuity. But you travel too, so we figured you'd understand." Then I told them what we had in mind.

Umberto replied, "We don't know much about the Bible, but we'd be happy to help you with this if we can." We met frequently over the next year, the four of us, to get a good look at Jesus through the gospel of John.

By the time faith was evident in Umberto and Doris, they had become ideal partners with us. I suggested they invite some of their friends, whom we had already gotten to know, to join us. When several of these couples joined us we returned to John, chapter 1, and started all over again. That was the beginning of a significant flow of the gospel to many people, continuing to this day, over twenty years later.

In partnering, we often need to make do with what we have. In this case, we started out with our children. Then, as things progressed, others joined us until we did, in fact, have an ideal partnership. The goal is for every participant to see himself or herself as a partner. Everyone shares in the ownership by using whatever ability he or she might have to serve the others and the group.

Two of the advantages of partnering are that it provides support and encouragement, and it allows for the pooling of our resources.

Partnering provides support and encouragement.

Two are better than one, because they have a good return for
their work: If one falls down, his friend can help him up.[5]

Partnering commits us to action. Most good intentions die of neglect before they're born. We resolve to do something. Then we get busy and the idea slips away from us, forgotten. Occasionally we recall what we had in mind to do. Then, a pang of good intention returns for a moment. But, again we are distracted. Thus our good intentions are soon forgotten and dead. Partnering is the best defense against such procrastination. It puts us on record. It calls on us to do the rudiments of planning. When are we going to meet? Where? For what?

A good starting point for partnering as insiders is to begin to meet with one another to pray, especially for our nonChristian friends. Ideas are born as we pray. And, when we pray over these ideas, plans take shape. Then we need to act.

Partnering allows for the pooling of our resources.

> From him the whole body . . . grows and builds itself up in
> love, as each part does its work.[6]

We have already observed how all of us, by God's design, are limited. Other factors, like time and energy, limit us as well. We might have only a couple hours per week of discretionary time. We are also limited in our experience and skills. Limitations such as these are perceived as insurmountable barriers—until we begin to partner. Then they are not a problem.

Both Mike and I travel a great deal. Our work takes us away from home as much as 50 percent of the time. That would be enough to keep us out of any meaningful involvement as insiders among our friends in our hometown. But we have chosen to partner. We have introduced each other to our friends and we work as a sort of tag-team. When I'm away, Mike is there to carry on, and when he travels, I pick things up. When we're in town together, we co-lead. In this way a potential liability has become an asset, as our friends who are being introduced to Christ have access to us both.

A surprising array of different abilities is needed just to bring eight or ten people together into a living room on a consistent basis. It takes prayer, coordination, communication, and hospitality. Someone needs to prepare to lead the discussion. The living room needs to be straightened up and the cups and glasses washed after everyone leaves. To attempt to accomplish this alone on a weeknight is enough to discourage anyone!

But when the participants voluntarily assume these tasks on a time-to-time basis, they become opportunities for mutual ownership. This is as important for those who are just taking their first look at Jesus as it is for the more mature in the group. Being a Christian is not a prerequisite to providing hospitality or coordinating schedules.

When we partner, those two hours of discretionary time we have available are enough.

Avoid This Trap!

THREE COUPLES DECIDED to partner as insiders. They declared their commitment to this idea by purchasing three houses in the same neighborhood. They envisioned relating to one another in such a way that their neighbors would be able to observe the difference the gospel makes in lives and then respond by joining them in their spiritual journey.

They began by meeting together to pray and study the Bible. Meanwhile they cultivated relationships in their new neighborhood. This went on for a couple of years. In time they met a woman who had just become a Christian. They invited her to join them, which she did. Together they prayed for her husband, and finally he too joined them. He participated in their group twice, and then he quit. Later, when they asked him why he didn't continue, he explained that he just wasn't comfortable in the group. He always felt like an outsider to it.

The odds are not in favor of success for any small group that already has a history together to transition from being a fellowship of believers to being a place where nonChristians will feel comfortable. That is because any group that meets with any regularity will quickly acquire its own culture. The members accumulate a set of shared stories. NonChristians especially sense this history and often feel uncomfortable with it. Their most common fear is that they will be embarrassed by their ignorance of the

Bible. They are certain everyone else in the group has already mastered it.

So what do we do? It is usually better to reconfigure the existing group into something new than it is to try to insert nonChristians into it. In this case, if one of the three original couples had invited the new couple to get together as a foursome, it might have been a different story. Insiders multiply, not by adding numbers to their groups but by dividing up to fit the needs of the people who are responding. New people need to feel they are participating in the formation of something new, that there are others like them who are also just getting started.

We often hesitate to dismantle our fellowship group because we fear observers will think we're failing. But it is not in our meeting together that the uniqueness of the kingdom of God is seen. That mostly happens as we go about living everyday life together.

CHAPTER 16

THE SIXTH LIFE PATTERN OF AN INSIDER: LETTING THE SCRIPTURES SPEAK

They asked each other, "Were not our hearts burning within us while he talked with us on the road and opened the Scriptures to us?"[1]

* * *

Nothing else is like the Scriptures. Our finest arguments, our most brilliant apologetics pale in comparison to the power of the Scriptures themselves in bringing people to faith in Jesus Christ. It matters not if the reader accepts or rejects their inspiration and authority. If he or she is willing to give them honest consideration, they will burn their way into the heart. That is because "the Word of God is living and active. Sharper than any double-edged sword, it penetrates even to dividing soul and spirit."[2]

If you have spent any time at all meditating on the Scriptures, you know what that means. You have had passages come to life right before your eyes. Through them you see something about yourself, or something that is going on in your life, and you know how to respond. A nonChristian will experience the same thing.

This power of the Scriptures comes from the Holy Spirit. They are his *sword*. And he tells us to pick it up and use it! "Take . . . the sword of the Spirit, which is the word of God."[3] We are to use the sword to defend ourselves from Satan's attacks, and in this case we use it to deliver another from his dominion.

Years ago when I began to share my faith, I was an avid collector of philosophical arguments and clever verbal exchanges to prove my position. I found I could always get a person to admit the fact that she or he was a sinner. But most people remained unmoved. I could win the point, but it was usually a guiltless admission. Then I realized, as I related in chapter 12, that I had been attempting to assume something only the Holy Spirit has the power to do. "When he comes, he will convict the world of guilt in regard to sin and righteousness and judgment."[4]

That realization resulted in a fundamental change for me. Once I began to understand the place of the Scriptures and of the Holy Spirit in drawing people to God, I saw everything differently. If the Scriptures reveal the truth about Jesus Christ, and if the Holy Spirit gives understanding—if these two work together to confront people with the ugliness of their rebellion and of their need, then my area of responsibility is greatly diminished. What, then, is my part? It's quite simple: I'm the friend of the bridegroom—and of the bride. I'm along to help the wedding go smoothly.[5] When I got this division of labor straightened out, I relaxed. Rather than worrying about whether or not people would get to the point of decision, I began to enjoy the trip with them.

GETTING STARTED

SO HERE WE are, seated in a living room, eight or ten of us. Most of us have shiny new Bibles, or dusty Bibles dating from confirmation days, or someone's extra Bible borrowed for the occasion. Whatever the case, most of them have never been opened. Now, you're "it" to guide the discussion. What do you do?

Your goal is clear. You want everyone to get a fresh look at Jesus—one that has not been embellished by traditions or preconceived notions. That is your goal because everything we believe hangs on one single question: *Who was that man, Jesus?* If he was God as he said he was, we have to deal with that. If, however, we arrive at a different conclusion, the discussion is over. Then we should all just shut our Bibles and go find something more profitable to do.

The basic claim of the Bible is that God has revealed himself. The apostle John, in his introduction to his gospel, said, "No one has ever seen God, but God the One and Only, who is at the Father's side, has made him known."[6] In other words, if Jesus was not God, then God is unknowable. There isn't any other that has ever come to us from beyond our time and space to reveal what God is truly like. John devotes the rest of his book to the development of this startling thesis. From that verse on, each paragraph, right to the end, adds another facet to our understanding of Jesus.

If and when we come to the same conclusion John did—that Jesus was God in flesh and blood—we must go on and ask the second question: *What does he want of us?* If he is indeed God, we would be fools not to take him seriously.

Actually, those are the only two questions we will *ever* need to ask as followers of Christ. In them our entire experience with God is summarized. Whether I am opening a Bible for the first time in my life, or am into my fiftieth year with it, those two questions are in order. Who are you, Lord? we ask. And, what do you want me to do? There is always more to learn about him—and our need for his guidance is constant.

It is important to keep this in mind as we sit with friends who are nearly at zero in their understandings of Christ. *We're* on the same journey they're on. We're asking the same questions. It's just that we have been asking them a bit longer than they have. You are not the teacher, or guru, as you sit there wondering how to get the discussion started. You're not there to dispense great wisdom to the others. You are a fellow discoverer, anticipating the excursion that is about to begin.

When we understand this, that we are all learners, we level the playing field. We are not teaching down to the others, and the others are not in a classroom, trying to get the answers right for the teacher. All of us are engaged in trying to see Jesus.

Starting at Zero

I USUALLY BEGIN by explaining that there are two parts to the Bible, the Old Testament and the New Testament. I explain that the Old Testament is an account of God's dealings with humanity before the coming of Jesus. The New Testament begins with four accounts of Jesus' life. This is followed by an historical record of the first few decades of the church. Then there is a collection of about twenty letters written by various apostles. It ends with a panoramic view of God's present and future workings in the world—and beyond into eternity.

I explain that the big numbers on the pages are *chapters* and the little numbers are *verses*. Explanations of this sort assure all participants that they are in the right place. This is, indeed, for beginners.

People need to understand why we are not beginning on page one, with Genesis, as we do with most books. The Bible isn't just a book. It's a library of sixty-six books, written over a period of sixteen hundred years by about forty different authors. My part, I tell them, is to serve as the librarian. I can help them find their way around, but we will be doing the discovery work together.

I select a book and explain why I'm picking that one. There are many good starting places. I've used Genesis, Matthew, Mark, John, and Romans. Certainly there are many others. Start wherever you are most comfortable. I am most comfortable with the gospel of John for the reasons I have already given. I also explain that John's book was written for our purposes. He wrote, "These are written that you may believe that Jesus is the Christ, the Son of God, and that by believing you may have life in his name."[7] John was a close, personal friend of Jesus. He called himself "the disciple whom Jesus loved."[8] Through him we get an intimate, firsthand look at Jesus' life and teachings.

FACILITATING THE DISCUSSION

IT DOESN'T TAKE long for people to figure out the house rules for a group such as this. They pick them up instinctively. *Can I ask questions?* they wonder. *What if I don't understand something? Can I say something without sounding stupid? What if I don't agree with somebody? What if I don't agree with the Bible on something? Is that out of bounds? Can I bring up a personal issue?*

After just a couple of sessions every one of those questions is answered in everyone's mind. From then on, the group plays by those rules, for better or for worse. So we want to set the right tone at the start.

Most people expect you to give a little sermon or lecture to start off. Surprise them. Once you've explained what you're doing and why, ask for a volunteer to read the first paragraph. Then ask a question. This is a decisive moment. Are you, they wonder, going to lead by *asking* or by *telling*? Because we want to lead by asking, we use questions to pursue the meaning of the text.

The next "decisive moment" comes when the first person ventures a question of his own. *How,* he wonders, *is the leader going to react?* Be sure you welcome the question. You can often turn it back to the group for them to discuss. Send signals that questions are welcome, that it's *safe* to ask questions. Remember, you aren't the repository of all biblical knowledge. You're just a librarian. If you don't have an answer, say so. "I don't know" can be a very good response.

A common mistake leaders make is insisting on winning every point of discussion. You don't have to get people to agree with you. You don't even have to get them to believe the Bible. Your part is done when they have made some sense of the text. From there on, it's the Holy Spirit's responsibility. If you feel you have to win, you will leave no space for people to think things through on their own. They need that space to wrestle with what they're hearing and seeing. It can be a long, hard road walking through one's own preconceived notions of Christ and on to where one admits he is Truth. Then they still face the biggest obstacle of all: giving up their rebellion and submitting to his *salvation*.[9] This journey often takes months.

PREPARING TO FACILITATE A DISCUSSION

THERE IS NO better tool than a good question for opening up the meaning of a passage.

Because the discussion consists primarily of reading the text a paragraph at a time and asking questions, your preparation should consist of enough reflection on the text to know what it says. Let it speak to you first. Then think your way through it, imagining the questions that might come up. You are prepared for the discussion when you have a half dozen good questions that can help people see what's there.[10]

So you need some questions. But even more than that, you need God's presence in the discussion. Pray! Ask God to give the group a look at

Jesus himself, that he will come off the pages and into view in the course of the discussion.

Keeping It Going

ONCE YOU GET started you will soon learn what works and what doesn't work in keeping a group of this sort alive and moving ahead over time. The following paragraphs summarize some of the more important things we have learned along the way.

Reminders

Be the *librarian*, not the teacher! Remember, you are a group of friends who are looking at the Scriptures together. You are there to help people find their way around, to find what they're looking for among the stacks of unfamiliar books—not to dispense information on whatever is being discussed. Be more interested in encouraging others to express their thoughts than in expressing your own. Let some of your observations go unsaid. But you can overdo your silence as well. Sometimes the group really wants to know what you see in a text or what you think about something. Then, be brief.

The size of the group is an important factor. If there are a dozen people, each will get only five minutes to talk in an hour-long session. Because some will be more vocal than others, that's just about maximum size. If the group gets larger—say it has twenty people—the communication style must change. You will have to go from discussion to presentation, and that's a line we don't want to cross. Most people can become skilled at facilitating a discussion, but few will be able to regularly prepare and give a presentation. This is one place where bigger is not better.

Keep track of the clock. Start on time. Don't let your preliminary, casual conversation eat into your Bible time. Quit on time. You may think you're on a roll in a conversation—that it's too good to cut off, but if you're going beyond the agreed finishing time, cut it! If you don't, people will feel they "can't afford another late night like we had last week."

Keep the discussion moving, and keep moving through the text. You can't explore everything that's there in a chapter. Try to cover a chapter, or half a chapter at least, in a session. If you get bogged down, the discussion gets tedious. Don't feel bad about not getting everything there is out of a chapter. You will never get it all! Your friends will see more the next time, when they take their own friends through the book.

Keep the hospitality simple. Serving food on a weeknight is more than most people can handle, and it becomes a hard act to follow. A beverage is enough.

Broaden the ownership of the group. End the evening with the questions Where and when are we going to do this next time? and Who can phone everyone before our next meeting to remind us of the time and place?

Keep in touch. Personal and telephone contact between meetings strengthens the bonds of friendship. An occasional social time is invaluable in carrying relationships to deeper levels.

THE LIFE SPAN OF A GROUP

THIS GROUP WE have been describing, like every group, has a limited life span. Most of us have had experiences with small groups that have served their purpose, but continue nonetheless, to meet regularly. A group is meaningful only in proportion to the purpose it serves in the lives of the participants. This group has been created especially for people who don't necessarily believe the Bible. Our purpose is to give them an opportunity to see what it says about life and its meaning. We, as the librarians, understand that this search focuses on the man Jesus. So we take people to see him. But it doesn't end there. We will explore what comes next in the following chapters.

CHAPTER 17

THE SEVENTH LIFE PATTERN OF AN INSIDER: MIDWIFING THE NEW BIRTH

* * *

We were in the middle of a discussion on chapter 14 of John when Jay commented on a recent discovery he had made. He said, "When you go on record with people who know you that you are a Christian, you take on a responsibility. They start watching you, and then you have to live up to that identity."

Jay's comment was a discovery for the rest of us as well. This was the first time he had told us that that he had taken that step. Over the previous eighteen months, about ten of us had been meeting to get a look at the Jesus of the Bible, pretty much as described in the previous chapter. Jay was the last of the group to declare, in one way or another, his commitment to Christ. I suspected he had been keeping that news to himself for some time.

The Scriptures are described as good seed. Peter wrote, "You have been born again, not of perishable seed, but of imperishable, through the living and enduring word of God."[1] Jesus used the same metaphor in his parable of the sower. In this parable, he adds two other variables that affect the prospects of our seeing a harvest: the condition of the soil (the person's heart) and Satan's efforts to take away the seed that was sown. "Some people are like seed sown along the path, where the word is sown," he said. "As soon as they hear it, Satan comes and takes away the word that was sown in them."[2]

This tells me that my job as an insider is to sow the seed, and *keep on sowing it.* I need to persist in my sowing while the Holy Spirit breaks up the hard soil, removes the rocks, and gets rid of the weeds that clog up the field. I need to keep on sowing until Satan's attempts to stop this work and keep the seed from germinating are defeated by the Holy Spirit. And as we persist, the time will come when this will happen. "A man scatters seed on the ground. Night and day, whether he sleeps or gets up, the seed sprouts and grows, though he does not know how. All by itself the soil produces grain — first the stalk, then the head, then the full kernel in the head. As soon as the grain is ripe, he puts the sickle to it, because the harvest has come."[3] With Jay, it was eighteen months between the first planting and the harvest.

Reaping true spiritual fruit calls for patience. Where there is a pregnancy, there will be a birth — if there is patience. Abortions happen where there is impatience. I learned this the hard way. I didn't always wait for the fruit to mature and come on its own. I was more inclined to go pick it, ready or not.

Dick and I met Hal on a Navy base. I was coaching Dick, also a Navy man and a new Christian, in how to share his faith. We struck up a conversation with Hal and found he had been thinking about spiritual things. When we invited him to be our guest at a breakfast where some of our friends would be telling their stories of how they had come to know God, he accepted.

On the morning of the breakfast, the three of us met at the restaurant and sat together. When it was over I turned to Hal to get his reaction to what he had heard. He was obviously intrigued. The three of us made our way to my house, where we opened the Bible together. I explained to him how to pray to invite Christ into his life. We prayed together and Hal, with tears, prayed as I had instructed him. That was the last I ever saw of Hal.

We tried for several weeks to reconnect with Hal in order to follow through and help him grow. But he kept his distance. Occasionally Dick would see him on the base, but it was obvious he was avoiding any further contact with us. I was puzzled; this was not supposed to happen. In fact, it was the opposite of what should have happened. When a person puts his faith in Christ, a special bond is usually formed between that person and those who helped him make that step. *What had happened*, I wondered, *with Hal?*

This question loomed in my mind because Hal was one of several people I had led to make a decision who had responded in this fashion. He was part of a very disturbing pattern for me. This incident took place forty years ago, and I have been pursuing the answer to this question ever since. The manner in which Jay's spiritual birth took place reflects the lessons I have learned over those years.

WHAT IS CONVERSION?

WE HAVE LEARNED that conversion occurs where a person entrusts himself or herself to Christ in such a way that he, in turn, entrusts himself to that person. John records that "many people saw the miraculous signs he was doing and believed in his name. But Jesus would not entrust himself to them . . . for he knew what was in a man."[4]

Jesus did not entrust himself to people who, in their hearts, were not entrusting themselves to him. They believed, in a fashion, but it was not the kind of belief that gave him anything to work with in their lives. They were not dealing with the basic issue that separated them from God: their rebellion. Isaiah's description of this problem couldn't be more succinct. He wrote, "We all, like sheep, have gone astray, each of us has turned to his own way."[5] Conversion demands a choice to end one's rebellion against God. If we want him in our life, we must be willing to end the war, to come out with our hands up. This is hard on one's ego, and that's why it's difficult. That's also why it can take months, often years, for a person to decide to take this vital step.

Our popular notion of conversion is very different from this. Our focus tends to be on the *act* of making the decision rather than on the submission of the heart to Christ. Many churches and mission organizations orient their programs around calling people to visibly perform the act. And many seem to be satisfied when people signal, in one way or another, that they have done it. As a result, over the past several decades, thousands of conversions have been recorded in country after country all over the world, but often with minimal enduring results.

Some of the most treacherous places in the world report up to 80 percent of their populations as being "born again." Lagos, Nigeria, is one example. The church in the country of Rwanda is another. It grew from being 10 percent of the population to 80 percent within seventy years, from the 1930s to the year 2000.[6] Yet a recent report from the Associated Press reveals that in Rwanda, 1,074,017 people—one-seventh of the tiny central African country's population—were killed in a genocide during the early 1990s.[7] Obviously, the many conversions recorded over the seventy years did not moderate the bitterness between the two warring tribes—the Tutsis and the Hutus.

What are we to make of this? Is not the gospel "the power of God for the salvation of everyone who believes"?[8] If 80 percent of Rwanda's population had truly experienced conversion, it would be one of the safest places in the world rather than one of the most dangerous. Similar stories of church growth that seems to have little effect on the lives of the people entering the church can be found in many parts of the world. This can also apply to the United States, where a large percentage of the population claims to have had a "born-again" experience.

A part of our problem is that our understanding of conversion has been conditioned by our culture. The church picked up on the message of the revivalists of a century ago—that people need to make a decision for Christ. But even a truth as foundational as this can be distorted. When, some years later, the business model—with its emphasis on measurable objectives—became the operational mode for the church, counting converts became inevitable. They are easy to count. This put pressure on churches and ministries to produce numbers of converts as proof of their effectiveness. In many situations our gospel has lost its purity under this pressure. We have reduced it to fit within the clockwork systems of our modern institutions.

Over the past several decades, church-growth theory has come to view the church as a social institution that can be planted, marketed, and managed pretty much in the same way it is done in business and commerce. Our consumer mentality feeds this trend. We will shop for a church just as we might shop for groceries or an investment broker. Where, we ask, will we get the best service? So, churches and ministries end up competing for market share! They too think in terms of potential customers, and their success is measured accordingly. Donors look for "cost-results" when they consider where to give their money. Because decisions (as we define them) and church attendance can be tabulated with relative ease, they have become the *de facto* measure of a church's success or failure. But in our haste to post good numbers, we are not willing to take the time to lay foundations that will endure in people— foundations that will, over time, transform their lives.

Natural Births

TRUE SPIRITUAL CONVERSION is an event that occurs within a process in which God draws a person to himself. He continues to draw as the person continues to respond. Sometimes everything appears to stop for months or years. God never violates a person's will. But it's like a pregnancy. We, as midwives to this process, need to patiently and attentively observe the progress. When we get anxious or impatient and act precipitately, we risk a stillbirth. Most often, when a person is engaged in an exploration of the Scriptures, the birth will occur without our help. The new life will just be there one day, obvious to all. Sometimes we will need to lend a hand, as we did with Jerry and Donna.

We could see that Jerry and Donna were responding to what they were learning about Christ as we read together in a small group that met about every three weeks. Neither had had any previous experience with the Scriptures, but after several months both of them obviously understood and wanted a relationship with Christ. After one session I suggested to Jerry that we have lunch together. He liked that idea, so we set a date.

There in the restaurant, Jerry was quick to tell me that he and his wife wanted to have God in their lives, but they weren't sure how to proceed. I suggested they needed to make sure they were clearly embarked on their walk with him. Jerry agreed with that, so we set another date— this time to meet at my house so Donna could join us and we could open our Bibles. Then we ate our lunch.

On the next Sunday afternoon the two of them joined Marge and me at our dining room table, where we looked into the Bible to see what it says about how to enter into a relationship with God. We were in the delivery room.

Don't Stop Now!

ONE OF THE advantages of putting a small group together for the purpose of discovering Christ, such as the one Jerry and Donna were in, is that when a spiritual birth does take place, people already find themselves in an optimum environment for spiritual growth. They are already among friends with whom they are accustomed to interacting. And they are already getting some biblical intake. They are born into a little community.

In contrast, people who come to Christ through an impersonal program or event are often left without a clue as to what they need next or where to go to get it. Left to fend for themselves, they will sometimes drift into a church where they piece together an interpretation of what has happened to them. They take their cues on lifestyle by watching the other people and end up settling for much less than they should.

Conversion is the beginning of a new and radically different life. It means being born into God's eternal family and receiving citizenship in his kingdom. As Peter said, "You are a chosen people, a royal priesthood, a holy nation, a people belonging to God." We take on a new identity. The new way of life we are stepping into is brimming with purpose. Peter goes on to explain that God's intention is that we "declare the praises of him who called [us] out of darkness into his wonderful light." And he says that this happens as we live "such good lives among the pagans that . . . they may see [our] good deeds and glorify God."[9] We are called to live today as the citizens of his eternal kingdom that we are.

New believers need to catch this vision of what they have become—and of what they are becoming. And they need help in getting from where they are to where God intends for them to be. This will inevitably require some early healing—and then a lifetime of growing.

THE LIFE CYCLE OF A GROUP

USUALLY, A GROUP that has come together to make an initial exploration of the Bible will follow a pattern, a life cycle. Over a period of
months, as people understand who Jesus is and discover what he offers,
the focus will shift to the issues they are grappling with in their personal
lives. Almost everyone lives with pain and is in need of healing. Now
they see hope that something can be done about it.

Once healing has started, it is important to continue on toward
maturity. But we can't stop there either or we'll stagnate. Our pursuit of
maturity must take place in the context of a vision of God's purposes for
us as an insider. It may take as little as two years to grow through this
pattern—or it may take ten! It all depends on where people are starting.
As the pattern repeats, spiritual generations should emerge.

We'll briefly describe this pattern in the following paragraphs.

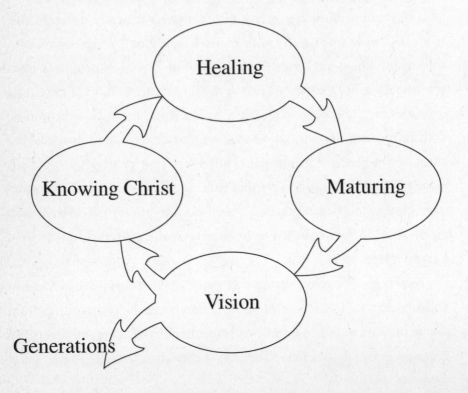

From Birth to Healing

As participants in our little group begin to submit to Christ, we need to shift from our first question, *Who was Jesus?* to the second, *What does he want me to do?* The focus changes. We don't need to break off from wherever it was we were reading together; we just need to begin to look at the Scriptures through the lens of this second question.

What does he want me to do? we ask. Jesus frequently used the metaphor of *light* as he addressed that question. He said, "This is the verdict: Light has come into the world, but men loved darkness instead of light because their deeds were evil. Everyone who does evil hates the light, and will not come into the light for fear that his deeds will be exposed. But whoever lives by the truth comes into the light."[10] Then he said, "I have come into the world as a light, so that no one who believes in me should stay in darkness."[11]

Until we believed in Christ, we lived in the dark, crashing our way along, getting hurt, and injuring almost everyone in our path. We still live with the consequences of those days—among the ruins of broken dreams, broken expectations, and broken relationships. But Jesus' coming is about healing damage of this sort. He said he was sent "to proclaim freedom for the prisoners and recovery of sight for the blind, to release the oppressed, to proclaim the year of the Lord's favor."[12] His coming was about healing broken people.

So what does he want of us? He says, Step into the light. Get this mess out where we can do something about it! Our natural inclination is the opposite—to try to exclude both God and the people around us from what is really in our heart. But there is no deliverance as long as we keep hiding.

Healing begins as we step into the light. That means putting aside the façade we hide behind and stepping into the open just as we are. It means choosing truth. That can be a terrifying thought! But that's where we need to go because we need healing and we need the help of our brothers and sisters. We are told, "Confess your sins to each other and pray for each other so that you may be healed."[13] Thus our little group can serve as the starting point for healing.

We are not talking about the group morphing into some sort of therapy session. This is simply a matter of being open about our needs for the purpose of engaging others with us in prayer. The healing comes from God in answer to those prayers.

Our first hurdle can be prayer itself. So far, we haven't prayed as a group. Because praying makes little sense to those who have yet to conclude God exists, we have not included prayer as a part of our sessions to this point. The idea of praying, especially in the presence of others, is often frightening. So we discuss our needs and we look at what Jesus tells us about prayer. Then we agree to pray for one another. The next time we meet, we get an update.

When we begin to confide in one another at this level and to this degree, we cannot at the same time leave the front door open for new people. People will share confidences only where they feel it is safe to do so. They feel safe when they know they will not be judged for what they say, and when they know their words will not go beyond that circle — that there will be no gossip. We need to become a safe place for each other. The opportunity for including new people will come along later.

We are not suggesting that this small group should be a place where everyone confesses everything to everyone. That is unhealthy! We are saying we need to bring others into our life in order to be delivered from our sins. But many times it is more appropriate to confide in one other person who will pray and hold us accountable.

From Healing to Maturing

New believers could be described as immigrants into the kingdom of God, recent arrivals from the dominion of darkness.[14] As new citizens they now need to learn to live according to the ways of this kingdom. Because its foundations are justice, righteousness, and love,[15] these same virtues are to characterize the lives of its citizens. Our life is to be characterized by integrity, virtue, and grace. This will affect every corner of the person: the inner being, where our thoughts, attitudes, and motives reside—and the outer, including our relationships, our work, our use of time, money, and even our leisure.

Kingdom citizenship is such a radical departure from the ways of our society that there is no way for us to just blend in with the rest and go along unnoticed. That's the idea! Paul writes, "Become blameless and pure . . . without fault in a crooked and depraved generation, in which you shine like stars in the universe as you hold out the word of life."[16]

But this citizenship also raises the bar to impossible heights. Who could possibly attain such a standard? Anyone who is in Christ! The journey lasts a lifetime, but we take it a day at a time. We do it by learning to choose God's ways and relying on the Holy Spirit to give us the will and the ability to live out those choices.[17]

Natural births such as Jay, Jerry, and Donna's give people a healthy start. They already know the Holy Spirit is at work in them, giving them the desire and the energy they need to survive and grow. They have already experienced this. Once they understand more about who he is and learn to deliberately depend upon him to help them pick their way out of their old behavior patterns, their progress becomes evident to all.

True, the road is a minefield—and they will get hit—but God has given them what they need to finish the course as winners.

The Epistles were written to stake out this course we have just described. The book of Ephesians will take us into it. So will the books of Philippians, Colossians, 1 Peter, James, and others as well.

Because there will probably be some in the group who are still deliberating their decisions about Christ, while others are ready to go on toward maturity, we don't want to turn the group into a Bible study requiring preparation. This kind of study needs a different venue. The by now familiar pattern of exploring the text with questions can continue to serve the group at this stage.

Vision for Spiritual Generations

During the discussion one evening, after we had been meeting for about eight months, Jim said, "These sessions are bittersweet for me. I love this: being together with people who have become such good friends and doing something that has become as meaningful as this has for me. But it's bitter in that I know it won't last forever. I know we will come to the day where we will need to stop and go on to other things."

Jim was right. There does come a time when, no matter how good the fellowship is, a group of insiders will need to break up. They need to break up because their friends have been watching and want to get in on it. They need to break up because they are surrounded by a world of lost people, because the demand far exceeds the supply. There are not enough insiders to go around.

We have found we have to break this news early, even before most in the group have come to faith. If we don't, there is too much resistance against stopping. We prepare people for this day by teaching them early to be insiders themselves, among their networks of relationships. We help them think about their friends from that perspective — to take little initiatives with them, pray for them, and serve them. It's easier for them to let go of what we have together when their own seeds start germinating. The time comes when room needs to be made for the next generation.

LIVING
AS AN
INSIDER

Part Four:

INTRODUCTION

*When he saw the crowds, he had compassion on
them, because they were harassed and helpless, like
sheep without a shepherd.*[1]

✳   ✳   ✳

The traffic crawls along. We get to our destination and can't
find a parking place. We make our way into the store that's
having the sale, pick up what we want, wait in line to pay for
our purchase, and finally get out of there. Our patience is frayed by the
time we're back home. Crowds! We didn't notice anything while on our
errand except the time we were wasting trying to get through the crowds.

When Jesus looked at crowds he saw the people. He saw their pain
and confusion, and his heart went out to them. Why can I look at crowds
and only see the congestion?

The difference is that Jesus was unwaveringly clear on what life
is about. Life, according to Jesus, is about relationships. As we saw in
chapter 13, this relational quality is clear in Jesus' reply to the question,
"Which is the greatest commandment in the law?" His answer was, "Love
the Lord your God with all your heart and with all your soul and with all
your mind." He added, There is a second one that belongs with this one.
It is, "Love your neighbor as yourself." Then he editorialized, "All the
Law and the Prophets hang on these two commandments."[2]

These statements tell us that life is, indeed, about relationships—beginning with our relationship with God and working out from there into the rest, to every other person in our life.

This is another way of describing what it means to be an insider. As we have seen, being an insider is not just adding another activity to an already cluttered life. It is about *living our life from the perspective of this "Great Commandment."*

In this fourth and final section we will discuss in practical terms what impact living as an insider will have on our personal life, our family, our neighbors, and our church.

CHAPTER 18

LIFE AS
AN INSIDER

* * *

So, what has happened to Jack? Last we saw of him (in chapter 1) he was lamenting the "loss" of his previous twenty years. Now how do things look for him? His circumstances haven't changed. He still lives in the same house. He still drives to work at the same time. He goes through the same routines in his job and sees the same people every day, just as before. Yet everything is different.

Since Jack began to intentionally partner with God as an insider, nothing *looks* the same to him anymore. He sees people differently. Although he's at the same job, his work means something else to him now. He sees it as an arena where he exercises his citizenship in God's kingdom. After work he drives home just as before, to where he and his wife are shaping three budding shoots in the centuries-old family tree of spiritual generations—the one that traces back to Abraham. They are teaching them how to live lives worthy of their heritage.

Jack's search for purpose is being rewarded. He knows he has a holy calling and he's already engaged in it. What had to happen for Jack to progress from where he was to where he is today? That's the subject of this chapter.

Two Hours a Week and the Rest of Your Life

WE CAN DO everything we talked about in the previous section on life patterns of a fruitful insider in a couple hours a week—if we are teamed up with others who are investing the same kind of effort. Much of it can be done as we go along in the course of an ordinary day: things like taking little initiatives, praying for people, and serving them. It does, of course, take extra time to provide hospitality and engage people in the Scriptures. But even that doesn't have to average out to more than just a few hours a week. Time is, to be sure, a factor in our becoming a fruitful insider, but there is another more forbidding challenge that stops most of us. It's the *other* cost.

As we saw in chapter 1, it was at the cost of a *cross* that Jesus bore fruit through his life. And that is the price of fruitfulness in our life as well. As Jesus neared the end of his days on earth, he began to prepare his disciples for what was ahead for them. He told them, "The hour has come for the Son of Man to be glorified. I tell you the truth, unless a kernel of wheat falls to the ground and dies, it remains only a single seed. But if it dies, it produces many seeds."

Jesus was talking about himself. He was saying, I am about to die, and then you will understand who I really am. It is necessary that I die because if I don't I will eternally be just a single seed. But by dying, I will give life to countless seeds. (Two thousand years later, here we are—millions of us all over the world—fruit of that one seed!) Then he went on and applied the same rule to us. He said, "The man who loves his life will lose it, while the man who hates his life in this world will keep it for eternal life. Whoever serves me must follow me."[1]

This is strange language! What's wrong with loving one's life? Did we not just read that Christ instructed, "Love your neighbor as yourself"?[2] Isn't it contradictory to now tell people they are to *hate* their lives? What are we to make of this?

Much of our popular wisdom today opposes any idea of self-denial. This kind of talk bothers us. It's dangerous, we fear, to good mental health. What about the importance of having a good self-image, we ask? What about our responsibility to achieve our full potential? This sounds about as interesting as bad news from a cancer clinic! What is Jesus talking about?

We will find the meaning in the context of Jesus' words. He was using himself as the example. He was saying, I am about to give up my life—in order to give it to people. If I hold onto it, if I'm not willing to abandon it, countless people will not receive the life I came to give them. And, he continued, the same rule applies to you! The more you insist on keeping your life for yourself, the more barren it will be. But if you, like me, open your hand on your life—if you let it go—you will be enriched, now and eternally.

What's wrong with loving one's life? It is self-defeating to love one's life in such a way that it results in investing everything in the self. We self-destruct when we become self-absorbed and self-indulgent. An unhealthy self-love can be as innocuous as insisting on guarding one's discretionary time or private space for one's self. "Hating" one's life, in contrast, is to willingly give one's attention to people rather than to self-ish pursuits. As the apostle Paul said, "I will very gladly spend for you everything I have and expend myself as well."[3] Thus, there is to be a cross in our life also.

This is another of those great paradoxes we find in Scripture. This one says, To keep one's life is to lose it, and to lose one's life is to keep it. How does that work?

Here we are, tightly holding onto our life, trying with our little fists to squeeze the last drop of self-gratification out of everything. Jesus is saying, Give it up. It gets you nowhere and leaves you with nothing. When it's all over, you will be left with only your empty sense of loss. That's what Jack was feeling. When, however, we put our self-absorption to death by opening our hands to the people around us, we will know what it means to live! Anyone who has seen the positive effects of God using her to serve another person knows exactly what we're talking about.

Jack has weighed this *other* cost and has chosen to assume it. The responsibility begins as soon as he gets out of bed in the morning. Insidership begins right there with his family.

INSIDERSHIP BEGINS AT HOME

WHEN GOD CALLED Abraham, he said: "For I have chosen him, so that he will direct his children and his household after him to keep the way of the LORD by doing what is right and just, so that the LORD will bring about for Abraham what he has promised him."[4]

As we saw earlier in 1 Corinthians 7, insidership begins at home with the family, just as did God's call to Abraham. It begins at home because that is where we find the people God has entrusted to us in a special way. We carry an additional responsibility before God for them. As we shall see, the family is God's plan "A" for making his name known down through and across the generations.

With One's Spouse

When we first moved to Brazil, our goal was to birth a movement of the gospel. We settled in a city of about a million people where there was a federal university. The campus was our starting point. We were just a few months into our work when I realized my wife, Marge, was struggling with something. As we talked she helped me see she wasn't getting enough spiritual food to keep her soul alive!

I looked around and understood why. She had no place to go to get nourished. Back in Minneapolis, we had enjoyed the encouragement of a church. She was in a women's Bible study. And she could turn on the radio whenever she wanted to and listen to Dr. Theodore Epp expound the

Scriptures. But in Brazil there was none of that. *What,* I worried, *are we going to do?* Then I saw it.

God said, "Husbands, love your wives, just as Christ loved the church and gave himself up for her . . . to present her to himself . . . without stain or wrinkle or any other blemish. . . . In this same way, husbands ought to love their wives as their own bodies."[5] The preacher probably read this Scripture at our wedding, but I didn't get it at that time. I did on this occasion.

God was saying, Jim, Marge is your responsibility. Until now you have been outsourcing her care to various parties. But someday you and I are going to have a face-to-face conversation about her. I am going to ask you what you've done to help her become a person without stain, wrinkle, or blemish. I will want to know if you have helped this person I entrusted to you become the person I intended her to be.

I was shaken.

That was a turning point. Finally, after ten years of marriage, I assumed what God had intended for me from the start! But I needed the distance from the props I had been depending upon to even see it. Because I did finally see it, she has been with me heart and soul until this day.

With Our Children

The same rule stands for our children. God has assigned to the parents the responsibility for their children's upbringing. As the people of Israel were preparing to enter the land of Canaan, after a punishing forty-year detour in the wilderness because of their disobedience, God instructed them through Moses:

> These are the commands, decrees and laws the LORD your God
> directed me to teach you to observe . . . so that you, your children

and their children after them may fear the LORD . . . so that it may
go well with you and that you may increase greatly. . . . These commandments . . . are to be upon your hearts. Impress them on your
children. Talk about them when you sit at home and when you
walk along the road, when you lie down and when you get up.[6]

God wants our offspring to be godly. This is his first line of approach
in discipling the nations.[7] It is the primary avenue to spiritual generations. So he instructs us in how to go about this. He says, Make my ways
your topic of conversation as you *sit*, as you *walk*, as you *lie down,* and
as you *get up*. We are always in one of those four postures. What, really,
does that mean? Are we to conduct perpetual family devotions? That's
what my parents thought!

My parents were new Christians when I was born, and they resolved
to do it right. I nearly suffered permanent emotional damage from our
nightly family devotions, which I found interminable and unintelligible.
I wanted to escape, but my parents' lives carried the day. They lived what
they said they believed, and that kept me from rebelling.

Moses' instructions sound a lot more interesting than what I experienced growing up. He tells us to observe God's ways in every situation,
from every imaginable posture. That can only be informal, in response to
the occasion, rather than the deadening boredom of ritual I was familiar
with. We determined to make this our approach as we raised our children. And I personally determined to never bore my children with the
Bible! I had to find a way to make it come alive for them.

We had two goals in teaching our children to follow God. The first
was to help them make the Bible a familiar, friendly book. So I *narrated*
it to them, from Genesis to Revelation. Kids love stories, and I learned a
lot about the Bible in the course of the six years it took me to narrate my
way through it. The other goal was to teach our children that God's ways

work—that when we do things his way, life goes better, but when we do them in our own way, we court disaster.

One day, twelve-year-old Michelle came steaming into the house, swearing she would never again talk to her best friend, Berenice. I asked her what was going on and she told me about their fight. I wondered, to her, if the Bible has anything to say about dealing with her problem. We turned to Romans, chapter 12 and read, "If your enemy is hungry, feed him; if he is thirsty, give him something to drink."[8]

I glanced up at Michelle. Her eyes were wide. She asked, "You mean I'm supposed to feed my enemy?"

"Have you ever tried it?" I asked.

"Nope!"

"Well," I said, "don't knock it until you've tried it." Then I went back to whatever I was doing. A while later I followed a sweet smell that was coming from the kitchen and found Michelle baking cookies. When I asked her what she was doing, she replied, "I'm going to feed my enemy."

She headed off for Berenice's house with the cookies. When she came back a few hours later, she said, "Dad, it worked!"

Now, that's an enormous discovery! When we experience firsthand the wisdom of God's instructions for everyday life, we begin to trust him. Trusting him leads to loving him.

No one else can be there for our children at teachable moments such as these. As parents, when we stand before God, it won't work to blame the youth leaders of our church for our failures with our children. Our society draws us—sometimes forces us—into making trade-offs that take away from this kind of parenting. Often a job grows into a prestigious but consuming career—during the time our children grow from babyhood into adulthood. We need to examine these trade-offs we make that, in the end, can leave us empty-handed.

As an insider, ministering to our family lays the foundations for what follows. Through our family, our message works on out, beyond, to the people around us.

With Our Neighbors

Larry and I had both worked in Latin America. Now we were spending a day together at my home in Colorado. In the afternoon we took a break in our conversation to go for a jog. Because my next-door neighbor Steve is my usual jogging partner, I called him to see if he wanted to join us. He did. So Larry, Steve, and I headed for the trails surrounding our house.

In the course of our jog, Steve and Larry exchanged stories. A part of Steve's story is of how our friendship had resulted in his encountering Christ. At one point, Larry asked Steve what it was that got him interested in pursuing this subject with me. Steve replied, "I watched the family. I saw how they looked out for each other and supported each other. I wondered about that. I decided that whatever it was they were drinking over there, I wanted some of it."

Larry asked him, "Did you know at the time that what they were 'drinking' had anything to do with their faith?"

Steve said, "No, I didn't."

Steve's comment was a surprise to me. Our family was oblivious to the messages Steve was receiving from us. It made me realize how true it is that one's family becomes one's message.

It is important that our children be aware of their roles, and ours, in God's workings among the people in our life. We are, whether we like it or not, and for better or worse, always modeling before our children. If we appear indifferent about our neighbors, how will our children take the good news of Christ seriously themselves? To not reach out beyond one's private world is an inconsistency, a kind of denial of the gospel that our children will pick up on.

A DYING SEED, SOIL, WATER, AND SUNSHINE

THIS *OTHER* CHOICE we make as an insider, to die to our own preferences as Christ did to his, aligns our life with his eternal purposes. We
will suffer with him, but we will also share in his victory.[9] It is a poignant
victory! The prophet Isaiah, prophesying about Jesus Christ, wrote:

> The Spirit of the Sovereign LORD is on me,
> because the LORD has anointed me
> to preach good news to the poor.
> He has sent me to bind up the brokenhearted,
> to proclaim freedom for the captives
> and release from darkness for the prisoners,
> to proclaim the year of the LORD's favor
> and the day of vengeance of our God,
> to comfort all who mourn,
> and provide for those who grieve in Zion—
> to bestow on them a crown of beauty
> instead of ashes,
> the oil of gladness
> instead of mourning,
> and a garment of praise
> instead of a spirit of despair.
> They will be called oaks of righteousness,
> a planting of the LORD
> for the display of his splendor.[10]

The good Seed from heaven was sown into the soil of bondage, mourn-
ing, ashes, and despair. Out of this soil have grown countless oaks of
righteousness—people who have exchanged their brokenness for freedom,

comfort, beauty, and praise, and have provided strength for those around them. God intends to sow us as seed into this same kind of soil, to effect this same kind of fruit among the broken people of our day. How does this happen?

Good seed will germinate. Just let it fall into the soil. Water and sunshine will do the rest gradually, without a sound. That's too slow and uneventful to some—like watching hubcaps rusting or grass growing. We want *action*—something big, noisy, and expensive. But that is not the way of the kingdom. It grows among us, powering its way forward from life to life, from generation to generation. The small, the apparently weak, is, in the end, the most powerful. This *other* cost is a small price to pay for this return!

CHAPTER 19

HELP THESE PEOPLE!

* * *

"How many people like this do you know?" asked Don, referring to the insider.

Don is one of the people who encouraged us to write this book before we were even thinking about it. Now he's our editor, working with Mike and me as we progress through the manuscript. I was ready for this question because I had been asking it myself. You, the reader, are probably asking it by now as well.

The first impression is that there are very few. There are, however, places in the world where insiders are a natural part of the believing community. Most of those places have one thing in common. They are pioneering situations—places where the gospel had not gone before and where those coming to faith in Christ meet him through someone they know. Such people are spiritually born thinking as insiders. Insidership is one of the values of their believing community. We have been repeatedly amazed to see new believers who are just discovering the Bible for themselves, reading it with their unbelieving friends, and showing Christ to them. We have seen this happen among Hindus, Muslims, Buddhists, and even secular Westerners.

A Blind Spot?

IN PLACES WHERE Christendom is established, the people we know who are fruitful insiders often have obstacles to overcome that people in other places don't. Both the structure and the theology of our established Western churches are shaped by the legacy of Christendom. Christendom was birthed in the fourth century under Constantine, as the church and the state worked out a relationship that would be of mutual benefit to both parts.[1] Within this arrangement, as we saw in chapter 6, church membership came with birth. Because people were born into the church, there were no unchurched people. The task of a parish priest was to provide the sacramental and pastoral services within his parish. There was no occasion for individual believers to see themselves as insiders, as we have described them.

The traditional idea of a local parish continues to influence the Western church. This is not wrong, of course, but it is only half the story. It misses the idea that the church is apostolic, that we are sent as God's people into the world "on Christ's behalf."[2] We seem to understand this well enough in relation to our mission to the nations, but we are unclear when it comes to our hometown. There we tend to depend upon congregating to do it all, both worship and mission. Consequently, we continue to be at a loss as to how to act as God's people in the midst of our lost societies.

We have yet to recognize the unique value of insiders. They are the ones who are within talking distance of the people the church is sent to reach, yet they have little space in our ecclesiology. Why are there so few? we ask. We are amazed that there are as many as there are! They are there, but the odds are against them. Few are encouraging them to do what they're doing. Few of their leaders are saying, Stay in there. Give your attention to your unbelieving friends. We will resource you. Too often it is the opposite. The message they get is, Demonstrate your commitment by being here when the singing starts. Not only do we not give these people help, the pressures of our expectations make it difficult for them! Is this not a blind spot in our ecclesiology, our doctrine of the church?

A PROBLEM OF ECCLESIOLOGY

IT IS ACCURATE to say there are 532 churches in Colorado Springs,[3] where we live. It is also accurate to say there is only one church in the city, just as it is true to say there is only one church scattered across the world—and across human history. There can be only one "body of Christ." It is true that "The body is a unit, though it is made up of many parts. . . . God has arranged the parts in the body, every one of them."[4] These parts of Christ's body are engaged in a rich array of functions, performing his work. The work they do is diverse and they come together in many different ways, yet we all, together, are one body, called to the singular purpose of bringing glory to God.

There are no normative forms for the way the church does its work. The 532 churches in our town shouldn't try to look or act alike. We would lose something if they did. That would leave out most of the people in town, because the church would be ministering to only one kind of person. Rather than bemoaning the differences and worrying about how divided we look, we should give thanks to God for the rich variety. We need more of it, not less!

Our diversity is an asset—but it makes us uneasy. We often don't know how to live comfortably with it. For example, one of the things it enables people to do is to choose their churches according to their preferences. Is that good or bad? It's probably both. On the negative side, it opens the door to competition between churches. Our competitive natures do the rest. Because competition is good for business, we reason, it must also be good for the church. With that, we make the church something to be marketed. Thus we find ourselves in the unholy trap of competing for market share with the rest of the churches in town. It's hard to have "equal concern for each other"[5] and be in competition at the same time. This possessiveness is perhaps the crux of the problem for the insider. We want *our* people to bring their fruit into *our* local church. If we can't get past this notion, ministering as insiders will remain the province of the few who have the courage to go against the stream.

There can be no guarantee that the fruit of an insider's labor will add to the growth of the congregation that is acting as a resource for him or her. It will add to the growth of the church in the city—or beyond—but it won't necessarily reward the investing church directly. Many church leaders have problems with this. It helps to get the view on this from the perspective of the kingdom of God.

THE VIEW FROM THE KINGDOM

THE KINGDOM OF God was at the center of Jesus' teachings. Jesus called his message "the good news of the kingdom of God."[6] That's what his disciples called their message as well.[7] And it was Paul's message. He was last reported to be "in his own rented house [welcoming] all who came to see him. Boldly and without hindrance he preached the kingdom of God and taught about the Lord Jesus Christ."[8] The church is not the kingdom. The kingdom is the eternal, unshakeable rule of God over all that is, both visible and invisible. The Lord Jesus Christ is the King. We, the church, are citizens of that kingdom. One day we will inherit it!

When we preach the gospel and people respond to it, the kingdom of God invades their lives. They become part of the royal family. They are given citizenship. They also become part of Christ's body, his church. But they don't need to take on the ways of the human agency that brought them the news in order for all this to happen. The gospel of the kingdom begins to grow in whatever soil that will receive it. This is as true for Colorado Springs as it is for Calcutta, India. The gospel of the kingdom is the good news for all peoples. It cannot be reduced to the good news about one local church or another.

When we *see* the kingdom and understand how good the news of it really is, we cannot care whether it grows here or there—or whether we will enjoy the direct benefits of the harvest or not. It doesn't matter that it falls to someone else. There is joy in knowing it is growing and that God is using his people today as good seed for eternity! We open our hands and allow God to grow others, and us, as he sees fit.

Acting as a resource for insiders requires this openhandedness. Wherever the fruit of their labor ends up in the broader church in a particular city, as long as Jesus Christ is our message, it's okay. Some of them might come our way. Others will be part of something else. Still others will need something tailor-made for them. Whatever the outcome, the kingdom and its citizens—the church—advance.

THE NEEDS OF THE INSIDER

IT IS TIME we begin to give people who have it in their hearts to live as insiders the help they need. If such people are to successfully persevere in the things we have been describing in this book, they will need the support of their spiritual leaders. This takes us to the instructions Paul wrote to the church in Ephesus in this regard. He said, "He . . . gave some to be apostles, some to be prophets, some to be evangelists, and some to be pastors and teachers, to prepare God's people for works of service."

God gives gifts to the church in the form of people who are especially prepared to do certain work. An essential part of their job is to enable, or equip, others in the body in turn to do that same kind of work. As they minister, they are also to serve as mentors. Then, Paul continues, the body

226 Part Four: Living As an Insider

will be built up. There will be unity. People will have the "knowledge of the Son of God and become mature."

The outcome of this combination of ministering and mentoring is that "the whole body, joined and held together by every supporting ligament [people who are connectors between the parts], grows and builds itself up in love, as each part does its work."[9]

These words scarcely need comment from us, as they succinctly summarize our point. A primary task of our spiritual leaders is to enable each part, every believer, to do his or her work. This is what insiders need—help in doing their work.

What kinds of help do they need? Consider the following:

Insiders need legitimacy.

Frequently insiders, as we have been describing them, are not even recognized as being essential to the functioning of the church. They are often misunderstood and judged. Teaching a Sunday school class, for example, is recognized as a contribution to the body, but spending time entertaining one's unbelieving friends at home is not. When schedules conflict and the insiders don't show up for something at the church, people worry that they are in spiritual decline. The legitimacy of what the insiders are doing gets questioned. Because of this lack of understanding, insiders can feel torn between two worlds.

Insiders need a context.

They need an "insider-friendly" environment—something that is larger than themselves. We shouldn't try to organize them, but they do need companionship with others who are pursuing the same goals. They need one another. They need occasional opportunities to confer together and to learn from each other's experiences. Insiders can be their own best resource.

Such a context could take several forms: from an informal exchanging of e-mails to a quarterly gathering for a Saturday morning breakfast. It should be relational, not organizational, in nature. Insidership should not join the list of ministries in the church bulletin. When we turn something that is really a way of life into a program, it is threatened with extinction.

This context is important because, as we saw in chapter 4, insiders are to *remain* in the situation in which God called them. It is very difficult to persevere in ministering to our unbelieving friends when we feel we are the only one out there—that there is no one else doing anything similar. But where there are others, and where there are leaders encouraging all of us with the message, "Stay in there! We're for you, and we are praying," it doesn't feel quite so lonely.

Insiders need content.

Few people, if any, already have the experience and the resources they need to do the things we've discussed in this book without further help. Specific knowledge and skills are needed. Insiders need help, for example, in knowing where to take unbelievers in the Bible and what to help them look for. They need a very clear understanding of the gospel and of how to let it unfold over time through the pages of Scripture. They also need to know how to synthesize the gospel in a single conversation and how to leave people with a clear understanding of what to do about it. This requires certain knowledge and skills that can be learned, just as we learn anything else.

Insiders need coaching.

Insiders have one more need that most churches are probably not in a position to meet right now. They need coaching. Coaches are people who know the game and have the ability to break it down into learnable segments. They are able to equip and encourage and have the ability to affirm and correct at the same time. They can point out where a correction is needed and then help people make it while continuing to move forward in their efforts.

Tom, a gifted coach, tells the people he is coaching, "You take care of connecting with others. You take the initiatives. The onus is on us to help you with whatever you get yourselves into." This kind of encouragement inspires people to move out beyond their customary comfort zones!

Such people are scarce. If insiders are in short supply, coaches of insiders are even scarcer. To be effective, coaches should be experienced insiders. That is why there are so few. It will take time and deliberate effort to raise them up, so this need must be in our thinking and planning. We need to train capable coaches.

We won't need many; a few good ones can go a long way, but we won't get along without those few.

Who Will Lead Us?

THE NEED FOR pastors and church leaders who have the heart for this work becomes apparent. But as we can see, it calls for a kind of leader we're not accustomed to. As a church, we haven't done much of this kind of leading in the past, so the way forward will need to be pioneered. It will take courage. Pioneering always requires a special kind of courage.

We conclude our considerations with three suggestions for our present and future leaders to keep in mind as they pioneer the way.

1. Begin to live as an insider yourself.

Jackson is a pastor. As he recognized the need to lead the people in his church into engaging as insiders, he recognized the importance of his setting the pace himself—in his neighborhood and in building bridges to his neighbors. He and the other leaders in the church began to talk about *circles of three*. A circle of three consists of three friends who are not believers, with whom the believer rubs shoulders on a regular basis.

You choose your circle of three by writing down the names of all the people who make up your everyday life. Then you cross off the names of all the Christians on the list. If you have three names left, these people are your circle of three. If you have less than three, then you need to form a few more friendships!

The first time Jackson did this exercise, he didn't have anyone left on his list when he finished crossing off the names of the Christians. So he went to work on that. He invited some of his neighbors over for barbecues. He assisted another in coaching a CYO (Catholic Youth Organization) basketball team on which his son and the neighbor's son played. He went to ball games. And when one of his neighbors had a serious crisis, Jackson got involved. Now he is engaged in the lives of three of his neighbors.

This idea is catching on. The elders of his church devote a part of each elders' meeting to sharing the news and prayer requests about their respective circles of three. When Jackson meets with the local outreach teams, their first order of business is an update on the news about the circles of three of the team members.

Jackson's sermons reflect his commitment to people who don't know Christ. Because people know of his personal involvement, his example, framed in biblical teaching, communicates with authority. They know what he is calling them to do because he is modeling it for them.

2. Give legitimacy to the idea of insidership through teaching and stories.

The Scriptures, as we have seen in these pages, have much to say about our living as an insider. But as it is with any biblical truth, these things need to be taught. The Scriptures give people the freedom they need to break away from their traditionalism—away from the confines of their exhausted scruples. They give us permission to change, and they give instructions in how to go about it without ripping everything else apart in the process. Biblical teaching can open the way for action and can elevate the value of the insider.

Most of our communication about values is indirect. We may never talk about "values" per se. Yet, we don't have to be around a group very long before it becomes apparent what the group esteems as important. The subjects of conversation, the stories told, the choice of heroes, the notions of success, the use of time and money—all testify to the values of that group.

As a young Christian I was quite discouraged by the content of my personal testimony. It seemed so—nondescript. I had heard an ex-gangster and several famous athletes tell their stories of conversion. I was both impressed and discouraged. Because I had never even seriously disobeyed my parents, I felt I had nothing to tell. I considered robbing a bank to improve my story! I did not value, at that time, the fact that my story of faith begins two generations back, with a grandmother who was helped to Christ through a neighboring farmer. He was an insider. It's a marvelous story!

We need to tell insider stories. We tend to overlook the significance of the early stages of the process—the little things, the initiatives and acts of service essential to helping people in the early stages of their journeys to Christ. Because people often equate the decision alone—in other words, the reaping—with success in evangelism, we don't talk much about sowing. The story, we think, is not worth telling if it doesn't end with a conversion. But our little acts of sowing are specific expressions of obedience to Christ, and are of great value to God. We need to learn to value them as well.

3. Make space for the insiders.

The Holy Spirit told the leaders in the church in Antioch, "Set apart for me Barnabas and Saul for the work to which I have called them."[10] The mission in this case was different, but the idea is the same. The elders in Antioch were to send two men as apostles into the region of Galatia with the gospel. They did as they were told.

Insidership is another essential function in the mission of the church and we need to be just as ready to support it as we are to facilitate the sending of missionaries. As God puts this ministry into certain people's hearts and we see them become increasingly involved with their nonChristian friends, we need to open our hands and release them for this work. We need to revise our expectations for them. It will also mean facilitating their connecting with other insiders for mutual learning and coaching.

AND DOWN THE ROAD

ONE OF THE far-reaching differences between our current ministry practices and a ministry that is committed to serving insiders is that of *venue*—the place where it all happens. We are accustomed to centering our activities in our church facilities; but insiders need to center their work on their own turf, where their relationships are. Instead of everything supporting the central facility, the facility assumes the supportive role to the ministry of its people.

Insiders' work is low profile. It can be almost invisible, blending into the social landscape as if it were camouflaged. It's a little group here, another there, with people meeting at no particular hour or day, without any ritual. You can imagine how this low visibility serves the gospel in places such as Muslim or Hindu societies. But for people in societies accustomed to measuring their success by numbers, it becomes a problem. Our own notions of success, and those of others, can put us under pressure.

For most of us, size is still the ultimate measure of success. We are not successful, we feel, until we have a *lot* of people to show for our efforts. As long as we think this way, these expectations will exercise the ultimate control over our activities, methods, and, consequently, our forms. When we are driven by this value, we have given in to the temptation to seek our own kingdom, rather than God's. It is amazing what can happen when we let go of this and when we cease to worry about who gets the credit.

232 Part Four: Living As an Insider

We are journeying a road we have not been on before. We are seeing new sights, new opportunities, new possibilities, and new problems. We can only address them as we get to them, not before. As we are fruitful, we will need to adopt new forms to accommodate the people God gives us, and form will then follow its function. And this becomes a far more adventurous road—one that will take us into new experiences with God and with people.

T H E   I N S I D E R

NOTES

Chapter 1
1. Ecclesiastes 2:10-11.
2. Ephesians 1:1.
3. Ephesians 1:4-5,7,9-10.
4. Psalm 2:2-4,6-10,12.
5. Ephesians 1:10.
6. John 5:17.
7. Revelation 7:9-10.

Chapter 2
1. Revelation 21:2.
2. Psalm 2:8; Ephesians 2:19,22.
3. Colossians 1:13.
4. Exodus 15:18.
5. Psalm 97:1-2.
6. Daniel 4:34-35.
7. Matthew 4:17.
8. Acts 1:6.
9. Luke 17:20-21.
10. See 1 Kings 19:11-13.
11. Matthew 25:40.
12. Philippians 2:10-11.
13. Rodney Stark, *The Rise of Christianity* (New York: Harper Collins, 1997), back cover.
14. Stark, p. 212.
15. Both from Stark, p. 212.
16. John 17:4.

Chapter 3
1. Genesis 12:2-3.
2. Genesis 17:5.
3. Genesis 26:3-4.
4. Genesis 28:14.
5. Deuteronomy 6:2-3.
6. Deuteronomy 4:6-7.
7. Psalm 78:2-6.

8. Ruth 1:16.
9. 2 Samuel 7:8,12-13,16.
10. Isaiah 11:1.
11. See Acts 2:24-36; Psalm 16:8-11.
12. Galatians 3:16.
13. Galatians 3:7.
14. Galatians 3:29.
15. See Matthew 13:37-39.
16. See John 6.
17. John 17:4.
18. John 17:6.
19. John 17:11,15,18,20-21.
20. Matthew 28:20.
21. Acts 2:5.
22. Acts 2:47.
23. Acts 5:14.
24. Acts 5:28.
25. John 4:38.
26. Rodney Stark, *The Rise of Christianity* (New York: Harper Collins, 1997), p. 3.
27. Stark, p. 208.
28. Stark, p. 115.
29. Ephesians 4:16.

Chapter 4
1. 1 Corinthians 12:27.
2. 1 Corinthians 12:7.
3. Ephesians 4:16.
4. Luke 19:10.
5. Matthew 5:13-14.
6. Matthew 5:13-14, MSG.
7. Matthew 5:16.
8. Matthew 6:1.
9. See Matthew 5:44.
10. See Luke 14:13-14.
11. See Matthew 22:39.

12. Mark 1:17.
13. Mark 5:19.
14. See Matthew 13:24-30,36-43.
15. Luke 15:2.
16. See Matthew 18:17. The Roman Senate contracted out their tax collection to individuals or corporations that would pay a sum into the treasury and would then subcontract local collectors to extract the money. Customs collectors were called *publicani*. They were notorious for their arbitrary and dishonest methods, harassing and even extorting money from the merchants. They were considered traitors. *Unger's Bible Dictionary* (Chicago: Moody Press, 1957), pp. 1254, 1255.
17. Mark 2:16.
18. Philippians 2:14-16.
19. 1 Corinthians 7:12-13,16-18,20-21,24.
20. Philippians 2:16.
21. 2 Corinthians 6:17.
22. 1 Corinthians 15:33.
23. Jim Petersen, *Living Proof* (Colorado Springs, Colo.: NavPress, 1989). See chapter 5.
24. John 17:17-19.
25. See Romans 14:1-12.

Chapter 5

1. Dates of Spanish Inquisition: 1478–1865.
2. See Luke 10:1-9.
3. Mark 2:2.
4. Mark 6:31.
5. For forty days after Jesus' resurrection, he appeared repeatedly to the disciples in Jerusalem. After he ascended, 120 people gathered in an upper room to wait for the Holy Spirit. Paul reports that Jesus appeared to about 500 believers in that period. Those are the numbers we have of people who actually put their faith in Jesus in the course of his ministry.
6. Acts 10:2,22.
7. Acts 10:24.
8. Romans 15:20.
9. 1 Corinthians 3:10.
10. 2 Corinthians 10:13-16.
11. See Philippians 2:16.
12. Ephesians 5:8-9,14.
13. Ephesians 5:15.

Chapter 6

1. David J. Bosch, *Transforming Mission* (Maryknoll, N.Y.: Orbis Books, 1991), p. 249.
2. Kenneth Scott Latourette, *A History of Christianity, Vol. 1* (New York: Harper and Row, 1975), p. 92.
3. Bosch, p. 244.
4. Jacques Barzun, *From Dawn to Decadence* (New York: Perennial, 2000), p. 6.
5. Several years after Martin Luther's death, after peace from a civil war within Germany was restored, the independence of the new sect, Evangelicalism, was recognized. Every German prince—every town—could choose either the Evangelical or the Catholic way. But subjects would be bound by that choice. Dissenters would be free to leave in a form of self-exile. From Barzun, p. 20.
6. Romans 1:17.
7. Bosch, p. 280.
8. Latourette, p. 1023.
9. 2 Peter 1:20, NASB.
10. John 17:3,8,18,20-21.

11. *Vines Expository Dictionary* (Old Tappan, N.J.: Revell, 1981), p. 63.
12. Darrell Guder, editor, *Missional Church* (Grand Rapids, Mich.: Eerdmans, 1998), p. 84.
13. John 3:28-30.
14. Ephesians 4:16.

Part Two: Introduction
1. Genesis 12:3.

Chapter 7
1. Hebrews 2:14-15.
2. Numbers 13:30.
3. Deuteronomy 1:28-30.
4. John 9:19-21.
5. John 9:22.
6. Acts 4:13.
7. Ephesians 6:19.
8. Colossians 4:5-6, MSG.
9. 1 Corinthians 2:1,3-5.
10. Ephesians 6:19.
11. Acts 4:24,29.
12. Ephesians 6:19-20.
13. Acts 4:29.
14. 1 Peter 3:15.
15. 2 Corinthians 12:9.
16. 2 Corinthians 12:10.
17. Philippians 1:20.

Chapter 8
1. 2 Corinthians 6:17.
2. 1 Corinthians 9:20-23.
3. 1 Corinthians 10:27.
4. Matthew 23:13-14.
5. Ephesians 3:6.
6. Galatians 1:9.
7. Acts 15:19.
8. Galatians 3:3.
9. Colossians 2:20-23.
10. Romans 14:1.
11. Galatians 5:19-23.
12. Galatians 5:16-22.
13. 1 Corinthians 10:32.

14. Romans 13:8-10.
15. 1 Corinthians 6:12.
16. Galatians 5:1.
17. Romans 14:14,17.
18. 1 Corinthians 9:22.
19. See Colossians 1:13.
20. Romans 15:1.
21. Hebrews 5:12.
22. Hebrews 6:1.
23. Galatians 5:13.
24. John 17:11,15,17-18.

Chapter 9
1. *The Matrix*. Warner Brothers, 1999 from www.whatisthematrix.com
2. Richard A. Swenson, *The Overload Syndrome* (Colorado Springs, Colo.: NavPress, 1998), p. 172.
3. Swenson, p. 51.
4. *The Matrix*.
5. Jeremy Rifkin, *The End of Work* (New York: Putnam, 1995), p. 19.
6. Rifkin, p. 19.
7. John 8:43-44.
8. John 14:30.
9. 2 Corinthians 10:5, MSG.
10. Swenson, p. 17.
11. John Stuart Mill, quoted by Robert H. Bork, *Slouching Towards Gomorrah* (New York: HarperCollins, 1996), p. 64.
12. Swenson, p. 111.
13. Isaiah 44:20.
14. Bork, p. 61.
15. Romans 12:2, MSG.

Chapter 10
1. Romans 2:24.
2. Hebrews 11:1.
3. 2 Corinthians 3:2-3.
4. 2 Corinthians 11:21-28.
5. 2 Corinthians 11:30.

6. 2 Corinthians 11:32-33.
7. Acts 9:20-22.
8. Acts 9:23,25.
9. Acts 9:28-30.
10. 1 Corinthians 2:3-5.
11. 1 Corinthians 1:25-27.
12. 2 Corinthians 12:7.
13. 2 Corinthians 12:9.
14. 2 Corinthians 12:9-10.
15. 2 Corinthians 4:7.

Chapter 11
1. Luke 17:21.
2. See Matthew 5:21-44.
3. Matthew 5:43-48.
4. See Romans 12:1-2.
5. Dale Carnegie, leaflet.

Chapter 12
1. Matthew 13:4.
2. Luke 11:10, AMP.
3. John 16:8-11.
4. Colossians 4:2.

Chapter 13
1. Matthew 22:39.
2. Luke 10:25-29,36-37.
3. Matthew 22:37-40.
4. Acts 20:35.
5. See John 12:1-8.
6. Luke 12:37.
7. Luke 5:30,32.
8. Luke 14:12-14.
9. See 1 Timothy 3:2.
10. Luke 14:13-14.

Chapter 14
1. Colossians 4:2-3.
2. Colossians 4:5-6.
3. *The Big Kahuna.*
4. John 1:45-46.
5. Larry King, *How to Talk to Anyone, Anytime, Anywhere* (New York: Three Rivers Press, 1994).

6. Colossians 2:3.
7. Colossians 4:6.
8. Proverbs 20:5.
9. King, p. 28.
10. 1 Peter 1:23.
11. For more on this subject see Jim Petersen, *The Church Without Walls* (Colorado Springs, Colo.: NavPress, 1992), p. 219.

Chapter 15
1. Romans 12:5.
2. 1 Corinthians 12:18.
3. Ephesians 4:16.
4. 1 Peter 4:10.
5. Ecclesiastes 4:9-10.
6. Ephesians 4:16.

Chapter 16
1. Luke 24:32.
2. Hebrews 4:12.
3. Ephesians 6:17.
4. John 16:8.
5. See John 3:27-30.
6. John 1:18.
7. John 20:31.
8. John 13:23.
9. Salvation. In the New Testament, salvation is regarded as deliverance from the power and dominion of sin. Jesus Christ, through his ransom on the cross, is the deliverer. Salvation is freely offered, but is conditioned upon repentance and faith. It is the work of God in us—which we submit to.
10. See Jim Petersen, *Living Proof* (Colorado Springs, Colo.: NavPress, 1989), Appendix: "Twenty-four Hours with John" for guide questions to the book of John.

Chapter 17
1. 1 Peter 1:23.
2. Mark 4:15.
3. Mark 4:26-29.
4. John 2:23-25.
5. Isaiah 53:6.
6. Patrick Johnstone, *Operation World* (Grand Rapids, Mich.: Zondervan, 1993), p. 472.
7. *Colorado Springs Gazette*, 15 February 2002.
8. Romans 1:16.
9. 1 Peter 2:9,12.
10. John 3:19-21.
11. John 12:46.
12. Luke 4:18-19.
13. James 5:16.
14. See Colossians 1:13.
15. See Psalm 9:7-8; 85:8-13.
16. Philippians 2:15-16.
17. See Philippians 2:13.

Part Four: Introduction
1. Matthew 9:36.
2. Matthew 22:36-40.

Chapter 18
1. John 12:23-26.
2. Matthew 22:39.
3. 2 Corinthians 12:15.
4. Genesis 18:19.
5. Ephesians 5:25,27-28.
6. Deuteronomy 6:1-3,6-7.
7. See Malachi 4:5-6.
8. Romans 12:20.
9. See Romans 8:17.
10. Isaiah 61:1-3.

Chapter 19
1. Darrell Guder, editor, *Missional Church* (Grand Rapids, Mich.: Eerdmans, 1998), p. 6.
2. 2 Corinthians 5:20.
3. Colorado Springs, Colorado *Telephone Directory* 2002.
4. 1 Corinthians 12:12,18.
5. 1 Corinthians 12:25.
6. Luke 4:43.
7. See Acts 8:12.
8. Acts 28:30-31.
9. Ephesians 4:11-13,16.
10. Acts 13:2.

ABOUT THE AUTHORS

JIM PETERSEN is the associate to the general director of The Navigators. He helped pioneer the Navigator ministry in Brazil, developed missionary teams in Latin America, and coached ministry teams around the world. Through living and ministering in many nations and cultures, Jim has acquired practical experience in applying biblical principles to life and ministry. He shares this in his books *Living Proof, Church Without Walls,* and *Lifestyle Discipleship* (all NavPress). Jim and his wife, Marge, have raised four children and live in Colorado Springs.

MIKE SHAMY has led the The Navigators' mission to U.S. metro areas since 1999. Through his ministry in New Zealand, Australia, and the United Kingdom, Mike has gained practical experience of what is needed to be an insider in increasingly post-Christian cultures. He and his wife, Audrey, now live in Colorado Springs, Colorado, where they seek to personally live as insiders as well as help others to do the same. They are the parents of four adult children.

Be a light to those around you.

The Insider Workbook
Jim Petersen and Mike Shamy
ISBN-13: 978-1-57683-420-6

This easy-to-use study guide and workbook will help you apply what you learn in *The Insider.*

Living Proof
Jim Petersen
ISBN-13: 978-0-89109-561-3

Evangelism is more than just a sweaty-palmed speech to a stranger on the street. It should begin with a life-style that is *Living Proof.*

Lifestyle Discipleship
Jim Petersen
ISBN-13: 978-1-60006-211-7

"Behavior begins with values, and values stem from a person's worldview. Until discipleship speaks to people at that level, there will be very little spiritual growth to speak of." (excerpt from the book)